hoot his documentaries. But a professional-strength editing system is never far away. Presenting Final Cut Pro®
nd output your footage anywhere. Whether you're on the plains of Africa, or on your couch at home.

THE FOLLOWING CONTENTS OF **"FLIPS 8 : MOVIEW"** WERE EXCLUSIVELY SELECTED FOR

ALL MOVIE-GOERS

BY THE PUBLISHER OF INTERNATIONAL dESIGNERS NETWORK

HOUSE 1 : DRAMA

HOUSE 2 : FANTASY

HOUSE 3 : SCI-FI

HOUSE 4 : DOCUMENTARY

HOUSE 5 : EXPERIMENTAL

INTRODUCTION

All around the world, at any particular moment, millions of people are watching images flickering across a screen.
It could be a TV screen in a cosy living room, a computer screen in an office or bedroom, a big screen in an airconditioned theatre,
a makeshift screen in a village square, a small screen in a college classroom. Whatever the channel and whatever the genre,
moving pictures are probably the most influential medium of our time.

The technical process is fairly straightforward: a continuous sequence of transparent still photographs, in black-and-white or colour,
is exposed onto long strips of specially treated cellulose acetate and projected in rapid succession onto a screen to give the optical illusion of motion.

The camera that captures these images comprises a lens used for focusing an inverted image of the subject on the film
while it is exposed; a shutter for regulating the exposure and blocking the lens while the film is being transported past the lens; a channel,
called the film gate, through which the film passes for exposure; and a mechanism for transporting the film through the camera
and past the film gate's aperture, through which the film is exposed.

There, however, the similarities between different types of film end. What the director does with this technique is as individual as what an author does
with a pad of paper and a pencil, or a computer. Or a singer with his/her voice, a painter with a paintbrush, a musician with an instrument.

Fantasy, sci-fi, animation. Documentary, educational, experimental. Mainstream "movie" entertainment or high-art "film". Short or full-length
feature. Commercial or MTV. The genre comes in all shapes and sizes. In this issue of *FLIPS*, called *Moview*, we examine some of the lesser-known
aspects of film-making – in particular, those talented individuals who shoot their own movies, often without benefit of cast and crew,
for downloading onto computers or, increasingly, for showing at proliferating "short film" festivals around the globe.

And those companies who specialise in specific parts of a film, notably the opening title sequences (as well as trailers and the special-features sections of DVDs). Those opening credits are as important to the success of a movie these days as a good headline is to the front page of a newspaper or an eye-catching cover for a book. And though they may only last for a few minutes, producing them can take weeks or months of work. Of course, borderlines are constantly being crossed – people who start out making MTVs for bands often move into the world of TV commercials and vice versa, likewise the title-sequence specialists. And all or any of them are quite capable of making their own short movies – and even of graduating to the production of full-fledged feature films.

With the easy-to-use software available today, making a movie, even a simple "home movie", is nowhere near as daunting a process as it once was. Almost anyone can do it. Whether anyone would want to view the result is another matter entirely. That's a question of meticulous technique, hard work, talent – and inspiration. We can't do much about the first three, but we hope that after you have studied the work of the artists presented in this issue of *FLIPS*, and read what they have to say about the subject, you will be inspired to follow their example. Or at least have a deeper insight into what they do – and therefore be able to enjoy it more fully.

HOUSE 1 : DRAMA

The word "drama" comes from the Greek word meaning "act". Almost all movies could be categorised as drama, but in cinematic terms, it has come to mean a film in which the performance of the actors, and the emotions they portray, are the paramount elements. Very often, cinema "dramas" are adapted from stage plays or novels. And although they usually attempt to be true-to-life, the stories are often written in such a way as to convey a particular opinion or idea. Through the abilities of the actors and the skill of the story-tellers, they aim to get the audience to sympathise with the film's point of view. The audience reaction most commonly looked for is: "What would I do in that situation?" And by use of another Ancient Greek technique, called "catharsis", they actively seek to arouse anger or love, and to provoke tears or laughter.

HOUSE 1 : DRAMA

CATCH ME IF YOU CAN

> NEXUS PRODUCTIONS LTD

SEE ALSO :

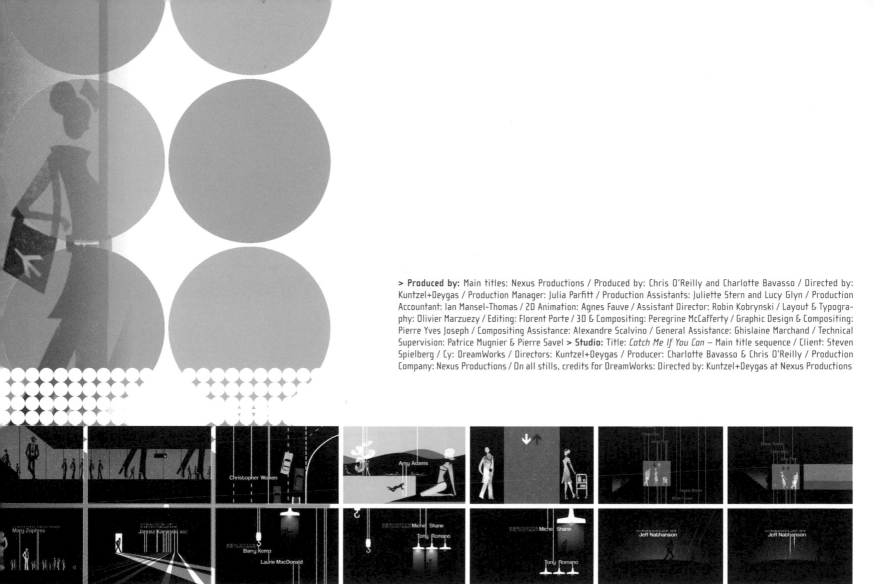

> **Produced by:** Main titles: Nexus Productions / Produced by: Chris O'Reilly and Charlotte Bavasso / Directed by: Kuntzel+Deygas / Production Manager: Julia Parfitt / Production Assistants: Juliette Stern and Lucy Glyn / Production Accountant: Ian Mansel-Thomas / 2D Animation: Agnes Fauve / Assistant Director: Robin Kobrynski / Layout & Typography: Olivier Marzuezy / Editing: Florent Porte / 3D & Compositing: Peregrine McCafferty / Graphic Design & Compositing: Pierre Yves Joseph / Compositing Assistance: Alexandre Scalvino / General Assistance: Ghislaine Marchand / Technical Supervision: Patrice Mugnier & Pierre Savel > **Studio:** Title: *Catch Me If You Can* – Main title sequence / Client: Steven Spielberg / Cy: DreamWorks / Directors: Kuntzel+Deygas / Producer: Charlotte Bavasso & Chris O'Reilly / Production Company: Nexus Productions / On all stills, credits for DreamWorks: Directed by: Kuntzel+Deygas at Nexus Productions

> NEXUS PRODUCTIONS LTD

Nexus is an independent animation production company with an international acclaimed roster of directing talent. Founded by producers Chris O'Relly and Charlotte Bavasso their first commission was in 1997 for U2's 'POP MART' producing animation for the world's largest TV.

Since then their credits have ranged across film, TV series, commercials, music videos and title sequences with a strong emphasis on storytelling and design exvellence, while working with the very best home grown talent, but also directors from as far-a-field as Tokyo, Stockholm and Paris.

Notable credits include the animated titles to Spielberg's *Catch Me If You Can* and the opening to Universal / Working Title's *Thunderbirds*. They have also designed and directed sketches for the upcoming DreamWorks / Paramount feature *Lemony Snickett* starring Jim Carey and are developing work for the new *Pink Panther feature* for MGM.

IdN: Most of your works are animated, why have you chosen this specific presentation?

NP: Never work with kids, animals, or any other lifeforms. I'm actually not sure we made conscious decisions to become animators, we both started off as graphic designer/illustrators, then thought wouldn't it be nice if our stuff sort of moved around a bit.

IdN: What would be the fun part making an opening title?

NP: The writing and storyboarding of any job is always the most fun. Finding ways to reveal the credits without the entire sequence grinding to a halt. There's a very delicate balance between allowing time to read the credit and keeping the flow and momentum going. With ads you have to end with the required pack shot, in promos you can usually do just about anything but the difference with title sequences is that there's information to get across throughout.

IdN: What is your favourite movie?

NP: Tough one. *Life of Brian* is hard to beat, Woody Allen in his 70's pomp, but I'd have to say, for sheer artistic audacity, it's got to be *Wife Swap Orgy 3*.

IdN: How and where would be your favourite place for your works' screening?

NP: Our first job was for U2's Popmart Tour on the largest TV ever built. It was fun watching it screened in front of 100,000 people with a few cheeky beers and an enormous PA system blaring out.

HOUSE 1 : DRAMA
CELLPHONES

> GREGORY BRUNKALLA

SEE ALSO :
> MURALS 102
> STRANGLER 054
> SKATIN' 050

Two girls chat on their cell phones about boys just as a boy interrupts, as a third caller, to read a love poem. My friend Anishika was staying with this family in the Bronx, I called her and told her my idea, and she said that I should come up and use the kids for the shoot. This was one of the more challenging shoots because I was the entire crew. I hauled a lighting kit, two cameras and sound equipment up to the Bronx on a Sunday at 7am. The girl on the chair is Gloria, on the bed is Leslie, and Michael reads the poem. I really just wanted to try to capture a realistic teenage telephone conversation.

> Direction, concept, camera, sound, edit by: G.Brunkalla

> GREGORY BRUNKALLA

Gregory Brunkalla is an independent
commercial/music-video director. His
work can be seen on www.brunx.com.

IdN: How did you become involved in Nike's "Art Of Speed" project?

GB: Nike contacted me via e-mail after seeing the "Skatin'" series on the Internet. This was a series of roller-skaters dancing in Central Park set to the music of Chromeo (Vice Records). They asked me to keep a similar sense of humour when approaching the Nike projects.

IdN: You have created 14 short films for Cornerstone Player DVD – why so many?

GB: Because Cornerstone puts out a DVD monthly, and I do all of their bumpers, so I end up with a lot of little pieces of work. These go on the DVD in-between music videos; I try to make series that contain at least three short ideas.

IdN: Describe your favourite movie-viewing venue.

GB: My favourite movie-viewing place is on my laptop in my bed. Pillows and DVDs.

IdN: What is your favourite movie?

GB: Right this second, my favourite movie is One Flew *Over The Cuckoo's Nest*.

IdN: How would you define the differences between film and movie?

GB: A short film is a snack and a film is a feast.

IdN: Where would you most like to see your work screened?

GB: My favourite place to screen my work is on the web. Even though the video/audio quality suffers, everyone gets to see it and getting feedback from around the globe makes it so worth it.

IdN: How do you feel about the growing popularity of short film?

GB: I love the art of short films. Branded content is obviously the big thing right now. And that's great 'cause a lot of us little dudes get a chance to shine.

IdN: If you could use specific items to represent the categories drama, fantasy, sci-fi, experimental and documentary, what would you choose?

GB: Drama – a broken glass. This is a very serious object and it could really hurt you. And glass only breaks when there is serious drama happening. Fantasy – magazines, they show you everything you'd ever want to have, look like and smell like. Sci-fi – a hoverboard from *Back To The Future 2*; I can't wait for them to come out. Experimental – bird shit, the remnant of true freedom. Documentary – spellcheck, a way to convert the instinctual into an actual language

GETTING AWAY WITH MURDER

> MOTION THEORY

SEE ALSO :
> RESFEST 2004 OPENING FILM 218

In the music video for *Getting Away With Murder*, Papa Roach sets off a stock-market crash, putting all of the dirty secrets and dirty tricks of corporations and politicians on display. At first, the lies spill out in the form of stock symbols: CHNY (Cheney), ENRN (Enron), HAL (Halliburton), WMD (Weapons of Mass Destruction), and more. As the market becomes increasingly crazy, we see a graphic of Florida glitching between blue and red, an American flag made of dollar signs, an F-16 fighter on a bombing run, wargames-inspired Armageddon on the displays, and a hundred other subtle moments that display another instance of "getting away with murder". Along the way, the stock market becomes increasingly chaotic, with stock traders giving in to their greed and passions, and the gluttonous stock-market bosses counting their cash, and breaking into the vaults, are caught red-handed, chased down and arrested.

As the band's performance intensifies, chaos increases – highlighting scenes of debauchery, explicit sexual encounters and political corruption – while highly politically-charged statements are seen in the video's electronic stock-ticker backdrop. In the blink of an eye, the insincere "In God We Trust" becomes "In Guns We Trust", then, more pointedly, "In Oil We Trust". In the final seconds of the piece, the massive stock ticker displays "Mission Accomplished", which then pulses back and forth to "Murder Accomplished".

The video was shot in one day (filmed on 35mm) at the now-abandoned Pacific Stock Exchange in Downtown Los Angeles. The ticker messages were executed using 110 shots with green screen that were composite to Motion Theory's designs.

> **Artist:** Papa Roach > **Talent:** Jacoby Shaddix, Tobin Esperance, Jerry Horton, David Buckner > **Management:** TBA Artist Management > **Manager:** Mike Renault > **Road Manager:** Denny Sanders > **Record Label:** Geffen Records > **Director of Creative Services:** Nicole Ehrlich > **Production Company:** Motion Theory > **Director:** Motion Theory > **Director of Photography:** Anghel Decca > **Production Supervisor:** Desiree Laufasa > **Producer:** Greg Jones > **Executive Producer:** Javier Jimenez > **Editorial Company:** Brass Knuckles > **Editor:** Lucy Mesina > **Design Company:** Motion Theory > **Creative Director:** Mathew Cullen > **Art Director:** Kaan Atilla > **Designers:** Matt Cullen, Kaan Atilla, Earl Burnley, Irene Park, Mark Kudsi, Mark Kulakoff, Gabe Dunne, Jesse Franklin, Robin Resella, & Daryn Wakasa

Full spread: *Getting Away with Murder*'s behind the scence.

> MOTION THEORY

Motion Theory, co-founded by executive producer Javier Jimenez and creative director Mathew Cullen in 2000, is a creative collective consisting of directors, designers, writers, artists, editors, animators and others. Utilising design, live-action and editorial techniques, the company produces commercials, music videos and other short-form works striving to create memorable projects that reach beyond simple function and form. The creative team has garnered numerous AIGA, AICP, D and Art Directors' Club awards. Clients include Nike, ESPN, Showtime, MTV, Toyota, Hewlett Packard, Warner Bros. Records, Geffen Records and DIRECTV.

IdN: Do you think MTV could also be considered as short film?

MT: Yes, we feel that MTV videos are one type of short film. Of course, some videos are simply short band-performance films, while others tell a story that relates to the song. Both MTV videos and short films involve heavy planning, stories and, very often, the collaboration of lots of talented people.

IdN: Describe your favourite movie-viewing venue.

MT: The Cinerama Dome in Hollywood, because it has a huge screen, comfortable seats, great sound, a long history, and you can reserve your seat before you get to the theatre. The only problem is that it's miles from the beach, which is where our office is.

IdN: What is your favourite movie?

MT: For short films, it's probably *The Powers Of Ten* by Ray and Charles Eames. For long-form films, it depends on the genre. But thinking outside of genre for a moment, *Wings Of Desire*, *Bladerunner*, *One Flew Over The Cuckoo's Nest* and *Eternal Sunshine Of The Spotless Mind* rank pretty high up there.

IdN: How would you define the differences between film and movie?

MT: Many people suggest that a "film" is more about art and theme, while a "movie" is more based in commerce and entertainment. But this distinction suggests that a "film" cannot be fun entertainment, which is definitely not true. So the categories don't always work.

IdN: Where would you most like to see your work screened?

MT: Projected on the side of the Moon.

IdN: How do you feel about the growing popularity of short films, and how can they achieve even more exposure?

MT: It's great that many people now have access to the equipment necessary to create their own films. We welcome filmmakers into the fold – life is much better with creativity, and the world will probably be a better place if people can find positive ways to express their individuality through film.

The most effective way to achieve more short-film exposure is for filmmakers to create short films worth watching. Now that it is very easy to make a film, too many filmmakers jump into the process as if it requires no thought. But most of the time, it takes an incredible amount of effort to create an exceptional project. Sometimes, people go through the process randomly, and the film turns out well, but too often, the film does not realise its potential, and the audience does not have a good experience. We all have to make sure that we maintain the highest possible standards for our creative projects, not for the audience, but for the integrity of the work. If it's worth making, it's worth making great.

IdN: If you could use specific items to represent the categories of drama, fantasy, sci-fi, experimental and documentary, what would you choose?

MT: It's very difficult to reduce film genres to specific items, because each genre covers so much ground. The core ideas that come to mind are: drama is emotion, fantasy is dreams, sci-fi is imagination, experimental is possibility, and documentary is not as "real" as people believe it is. They are all a journey, a slice of life that explores the human experience from a particular viewpoint. It may not be useful to create simple icons for them, because they are such complex areas of art. It would be like representing a whole style of art with only one work from one artist.

HOUSE 1 : DRAMA

IMAGINING ARGINTINA

> 4U+CO.

SEE ALSO :

IMAGINING ARGENTINA

ANTONIO BANDERAS

Executive Producers LUCAS FOSTER
ORDI BOS
LOURDES DÍAZ

Visual Producer KIRK D'AMICO
PHILIP VON ALVENSLEBEN

In Buenos Aires during the Peron era, an Argentine playwright has a preternatural ability to see what will happen to people's loved ones - many of whom are missing, or soon will be - when he looks into their faces. Ultimately, he must turn this power inward, when his activist journalist wife disappears.

> **Creative designer/director:** Garson Yu > **Producer:** Jennifer Fong > **Typographer:** Yolanda Santosa
> **Editor:** Tony Fulgham > **Client:** Christopher Hampton, director > **Distributor:** Arenas Entertainment

> **YU+CO.**

Established by Garson Yu in 1998, yU+co. is a motion-graphics specialist, providing high-concept design and production services for motion-picture main titles and trailers, theatrical logos, television-show opens/promos, commercials and network branding, as well as designing for emerging digital technologies, information architecture and websites.

It has created graphics for commercial spots by Nokia, AOL, Moviefone, Verizon, American Express, Motorola and Toyota, as well as for networks such as HBO, CNN, TNT, Anime Network, Showtime and ESPN. Feature credits include opening sequences for *The Last Shot, Wicker Park, Taking Lives, Paycheck, Matchstick Men, The Hulk, The Italian Job, The Recruit, Shanghai Knights, Spy Game, I Am Sam* and *The Others*.

Along with creative director Garson Yu, the company's executive team also includes vice president Carol Wong and executive producer Claire O'Brien. The newest addition to yU+co. is a visual-effects department, which includes VFX producer Petra Holtorf and a team of highly skilled Shake compositors. Some of their credits include visual-effects shots for *First Daughter, The Day After Tomorrow, Peter Pan, Open Range, Scary Movie 3, The Scorpion King, Godzilla, Stewart Little* and *The Grinch*.

IdN: People tend to overlook trailers and opening titles, being unaware that they are often produced by professional specialists such as yourselves. How do you feel about that?

yU+co.: The entertainment industry in the US always has specialist professionals to handle each aspect of a movie. Trailers are usually handled by the marketing department of the studio; the director usually has less creative involvement in making the trailer. However, for the main title, the director is the guiding light for the title designer to define the tone of the opening of the film. yU+co is in a very specialised field. We package movies, sometimes condensing a two-hour movie into a 90-second trailer. And sometimes a story into a single metaphor for a title sequence. I am proud of what we do because when I go to the movies, I truly appreciate seeing and hearing the audience's reaction to the trailers we create. Sometimes I even hear people comment about the opening title being better than the movie. It is not important to me whether people know who does it. Filmmaking is always about collaboration and I am happy to be a collaborator.

IdN: What is the most memorable opening title sequence you have created?

yU+co.: As far as I am concerned, the most memorable opening title was for *The Hulk*. Although every film I've worked on has had unique challenges and has ultimately been a pleasant and rewarding experience. Just imagine working with world-famous directors and going through their creative process! Each of them has their own individual philosophy and to be given the opportunity to work them is an honour.

For *The Hulk*, I was hired during the research and development stage as a visual designer for the film. I worked with Ang Lee to develop the multiple screens and a transitional-device technique, in addition to designing the opening title sequence. I was given the opportunity to direct the live-action part for the entire sequence. It was a seven-day shoot at ILM in San Francisco with Ang's DP Fred Elmes. What a great experience! The challenge of *The Hulk* opening was to tell a complex background story of David Banner's scientific experiment within three minutes. It was a complex choreography of images, mimicking the time-lap effects, condensing the events over time and setting up the tone and story. I thoroughly enjoyed the process as much as the final product.

IdN: What would be the fun part of making an opening title?

yU+co.: I always enjoy creating my own original materials for the title sequence. Shooting, editing and putting the whole piece together is the fun part.

IdN: What would be the most difficult part of making an opening title?

yU+co.: I find the decision-making process to be the most constricting. Most of the time we are dealing with many decision-makers coming from different perspectives. Some see the importance of creativity, some simply do not.

IdN: Describe your favourite movie-viewing venue.

yU+co.: A theatre. A film needs to be seen and projected on a large screen. I don't like watching movies at a mini cineplex. I would rather watch movies at home sitting on my favourite couch.

IdN: What is your favourite movie?

yU+co.: *The Godfather*.

IdN: How would you define the differences between film and movie?

yU+co.: They are spelled differently, aren't they? How about: a film inspires me; a movie entertains me.

IdN: Where would you most like to see your work screened?

yU+co.: When I was a little boy, I used to hide under a blanket to read my comic books with a flashlight. I also like to close my eyes and imagine things. I enjoy the dark. That's my favourite place. I would prefer to screen my work in a theatre where the audience is enclosed by darkness.

IdN: If you could use a specific item to represent the categories drama, fantasy, sci-fi, experimental and documentary, what would you choose?

yU+co.: Drama – a mirror. Drama is about people. It's about us. Sci-fi – a door. I used to stare at the door and wonder what's behind it. Experimental – a blank canvas. Experimental can be an expression. Documentary – an old recording machine, because it's non-fiction.

HOUSE 1 : DRAMA

KINGDOM HOSPITAL

> DIGITALKITCHEN

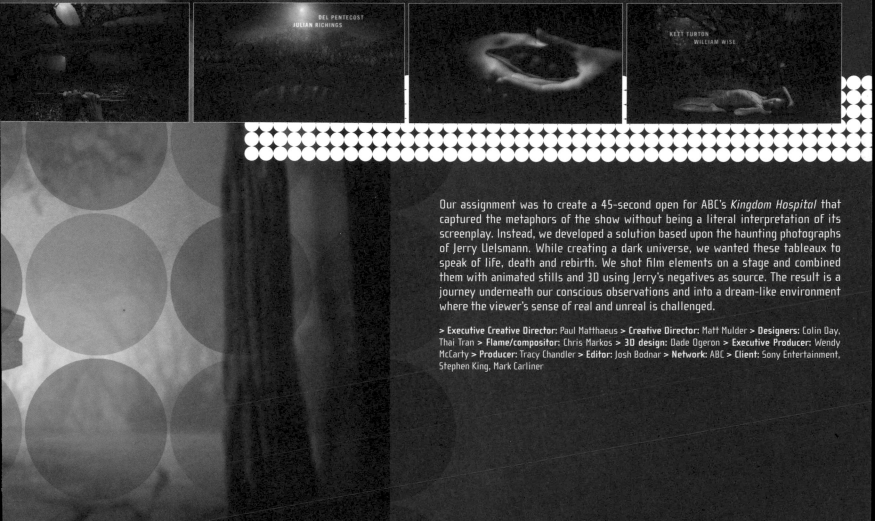

DEL PENTECOST
JULIAN RICHINGS

KETT TURTON
WILLIAM WISE

Our assignment was to create a 45-second open for ABC's *Kingdom Hospital* that captured the metaphors of the show without being a literal interpretation of its screenplay. Instead, we developed a solution based upon the haunting photographs of Jerry Uelsmann. While creating a dark universe, we wanted these tableaux to speak of life, death and rebirth. We shot film elements on a stage and combined them with animated stills and 3D using Jerry's negatives as source. The result is a journey underneath our conscious observations and into a dream-like environment where the viewer's sense of real and unreal is challenged.

> **Executive Creative Director:** Paul Matthaeus > **Creative Director:** Matt Mulder > **Designers:** Colin Day, Thai Tran > **Flame/compositor:** Chris Markos > **3D design:** Dade Ogeron > **Executive Producer:** Wendy McCarty > **Producer:** Tracy Chandler > **Editor:** Josh Bodnar > **Network:** ABC > **Client:** Sony Entertainment, Stephen King, Mark Carliner

> DIGITAL_KITCHEN

DIGITALKITCHEN was founded in 1995 as the digital studio for an independent advertising agency in Seattle, helmed by creative director Paul Matthaeus. In 2000, Don McNeill joined Matthaeus as president and executive producer. DK has posted double-digit growth every year since, while winning recognition in major advertising and entertainment forums.

It specialises in film and video production, DVD and interactive authoring, environmental, venue and event content, broadcast entertainment and celebrity affiliations, traditional television spot development and production and strategic planning, research and development

DK's work has touched over 100 countries and been featured in general and trade publications including *Time* Magazine, *The New York Times, Wall Street Journal, Entertainment Weekly* and *AdWeek*, and is part of the New York Museum of Modern Art Permanent Collection. In 2001, DK was voted best by the Association of Independent Commercial Producers (AICP) and in 2002, DK won an Emmy at the Academy of Television Arts & Sciences.

The company has produced and directed work for clients such as Nike, Chrysler, Ford, Chevrolet, Sears, AT&T, Microsoft and Sony, and entertainment content for Paramount Studios, Sony Entertainment, Columbia Pictures, 20th Century Fox, HBO, NBC and CBS. It has offices in Seattle, Chicago, Los Angeles, the United Kingdom and France.

IdN: How strongly do you think an opening title sequence affects the impact of the film that follows?

DK: Complex to answer really, because so much depends on the precise chemistry between the film and the opening sequence. Sometimes the open is a material contributor to the trajectory of the storyline. At minimum, there's an opportunity to create an emotional backdrop from which the series or film can unfurl. Too often, it's nothing more than labelling and a moving headsheet of actors. To me, that's an opportunity lost.

IdN: Are there any big differences in terms of production between making title sequences for cinema and for TV?

DK: Huge, really. There's a hierarchy of attention and viewer value – TV and in-theatre feature films occupy very different positions on that scale. TV has a much shorter attention span, and the entertainment asset is held to a lesser value set than films. Today, people watch TV very passively – in the kitchen, getting ready for work, watching from across the room. As designers we need to recognise that. In-theatre viewing is infinitely more immersing, and attention is relatively undivided. DVDs and broadcast feature films on premium cable are somewhere in between.

IdN: What would be the fun part of making an opening title?

DK: The conceptual phase – the connection to the human condition resides there.

IdN: Describe your favourite movie-viewing venue.

DK: My home theatre, unfortunately. Most out-of-home theatre experiences don't measure up after taking into account the noise and nuisance, with the possible exception of the cinema theatre here in Seattle.

IdN: What is your favourite movie?

DK: Of recent years, *American Beauty*.

IdN: How would you define the differences between film and movies?

DK: I wouldn't, although cultural associations are probably different.

IdN: Where would you most like to see your work screened?

DK: Because we work in the digital realm, I have to say that 2k digital projection is the best: sharp, smooth and brilliant. There are so many generations between the original negative and the print for theatre projection – clarity and tonal quality are markedly compromised. For that reason, analogy has become second best, sadly.

IdN: People tend to overlook trailers and opening titles in terms of knowing that a professional company has usually created them. How do you feel about this?

DK: I suppose they should garner greater credit. For example, the music composer has been credited in opening main titles we've created, where we have not. The casual viewer would probably think that we had a bigger contribution to the impact. Regardless, I'm not in this business for fame, so it doesn't keep me up at night.

HOUSE 1 : DRAMA
KITCHEN, CLEANING, PIANO TEACHER, TUXEDO.

> THE GLUE SOCIETY

> **Title:** *Kitchen, Cleaning, Piano Teacher*, Tuxedo. > **Client (Brand)/Artist:** Elle Macpherson Intimates/
Bendon (NZ) > **City & Country:** Sydney, Australia > **Creative Director:** The Glue Society > **Copywriter:**
Jonathan Kneeb One > **Art Director:** Gary Freedman > **Director:** The Glue Society > **Production Co & City:**
@RADICALMEDIA, New York > **Producer:** Annabel Blackett > **Director of Photography:** Mario Sorrenti &
Stuart Dryburgh > **Post Production & City:** Engine, Sydney > **Editor & Company:** Nick Foley-Jones > **Air
Date:** 29/08/04 > **Secs:** 10

> THE GLUE SOCIETY

The Glue Society is an independent creative group based in Sydney, Australia, principally working as writers, directors and designers.

The Glue Society has produced advertising campaigns in Australia, Asia, the UK and US for brands such as Virgin Mobile, Channel V, Elle Macpherson Intimates and Mercedes and for agencies including Saatchi & Saatchi, BBDO, Publicis and Crispin Porter Bogusky.

Founded in 1998 by Jonathan Kneebone and Gary Freedman, The Glue Society's work encompasses all aspects of communication, film, art and design.

HOUSE 1 : DRAMA
MIRANDA

> NEXUS PRODUCTIONS LTD

An animated title sequence for the British feature film *Miranda* starring Christina Ricci, Kyle McLaughlan, John Sim and John Hurt.. Award winning directors Smith & Foulkes at Nexus worked with a simple 'pixel' design more often associated with the net and worked it into a tense *film noire* narrative.

> **Director:** Smith & Foulkes > **Producer:** Chris O'eilly and Charlotte Bavasso > **Production company:** Nexus > *Miranda* directed by Marc Munden > A Feelgood Fiction/Channel 4 production > Produced by Laurence Bowen

HOUSE 1 : DRAMA
NIKE : OLE

> LORENZO FONDA / FABRICA

SEE ALSO :
> A GHOST IN FABRICA 082

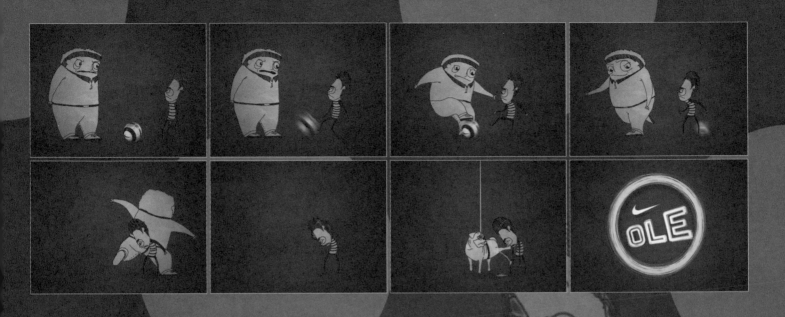

The agency approached us to create four animated short
TV commercials for Nike's PKO soccer tournanment. As
they were eight seconds each, we worked on quickness
and effectiveness of actions.

> **Agency:** Sartoria > **Production company:** thankyourupert.com >
Animator: Lorenzo Fonda (www.cerberoleso.it) > **Editor:** Enrico Mazzi
> www.dentenuovo.it > **Sound editor:** Olga Productions

> FABRICA

Fabrica is a communication research and development centre founded in 1994 by the Benetton Group. At Fabrica young artists and experimenters under 25 gather and develop their creativity and concrete communication projects in fields that range from cinema, graphic design, industrial design, music, illustration, photography, new media and editorial production.

> JOE TOGNERI / FABRICA

Joe Togneri, a native of San Francisco, California, is a graduate of New York City's School of Visual Arts. He began working in advertising as a producer at Grey in New York City, where he produced TV spots for clients such as Kraft foods, Proctor & Gamble and Post Cereal. In 1998 he moved to Arnold Advertising in Boston to head up production for the McDonald's account. While there he produced spots for other clients such as Dow Jones, which aired during the 2000 Super Bowl.

During a typical advertising encounter at a hotel swimming pool in Los Angeles, he met a producer from Italy who offered him a job in Milan. By the spring of 2000 the offer became a reality and he moved to Milan to work for Leo Burnett, heading up the launch of Blu Telecommunications and Fiat Automotive. While at Leo Burnett he produced a campaign for Fiat that captured national attention by the Prime Minister quoting the punch line of the spot in an address to the Italian Parliament. The campaign went on to win a prize at Cannes that year.

After Leo Burnett, Joe moved on to produce spots as a freelance for various agencies and production companies that included Publicis, TBWA/Chiat Day and Red Cell. He came to Fabrica (Benetton's communication research centre) as the TV/video department head at the beginning of 2003 to follow various projects for profit/non-profit organisations such as Reporter's Without Borders, La Fura Di Baus and Louis Vuitton.

IdN: How did Fabrica become involved in the short-film field?

JT: We are involved in this area by investing our time, money and efforts into developing and promoting our directors and their projects. Everyone who does a trial period in the video department for two weeks must present their ideas for future projects. It is a fundamental aspect of Fabrica that we maintain our presence on the short-film festival circuits and the student films are usually the ones that shine the brightest.

IdN: Who have you worked with in terms of Hollywood?

JT: Well, we have made big movies that have played to Hollywood, such as *No Man's Land*, which won the Academy Award for best foreign film. Outside of Hollywood, we would like to get into more experimental types of communications such as the work Spike Jonze did for Volvo, in which he created a fake documentary, or like Kessel Kramer's project with the soccer World Cup for the worst teams. These types of projects are really interesting because they confuse the line between advertising and art.

IdN: Why did you choose the three directors you recommended for our *FLIPS 8 – Moview*?

JT: I chose them because they are the directors most interested in motion graphics at Fabrica at this time.

IdN: Describe your favourite movie-viewing venue.

JT: An empty Ziegfield Theatre, fifth row back, centre.

IdN: What is your favourite movie?

JT: The little Super 8 films I created with my brother when we were kids.

IdN: How would you define the differences between film and movie?

JT: For me it's one and the same. I know what most people think the answer is, but I have seen many short films that have had more impact than a full-scale "movie".

IdN: Where would you most like to see your work screened?

JT: On computer screens across the world. I am fascinated by the short films that people pass via Internet between friends and colleagues. This is really a true test of devotion when millions of people find something you did entertaining while watching it in the worst possible format – pixilated and compressed.

IdN: How do you feel about the growing popularity of short films?

JT: With the advent of the technology being affordable, new filmmakers are recognised daily. I think this is really cool. When I was a film student in New York, a short film in Super 8 – I still love that format – or 16mm was really costly. Now I see directors creating very sophisticated work on their portable computers. This is the future and the paying public is starting to embrace this idea.

IdN: From your point of view, what would be the most effective and useful way to create greater short-film exposure?

JT: Well, the more the public purchases, downloads and rents short-film compilations, the more we'll see on the market. The responsibility to spread the word is really in the hands of the people who are reading this interview right now. Go and tell the world to support these types of work by buying compilation DVDs such as our self-portraits series and our 10-year anniversary book/DVD. Was that too shameless?

IdN: If you could use specific items to represent the categories drama, fantasy, sci-fi, experimental and documentary, what would you choose?

JT: Drama – green bench in Union Square Park where film students film their first dramas. Fantasy – a bright orange wig, Matthew Barney. Sci-fi – raw laytex, for moulding. Experimental – a vinyl record that has a visible start and endpoint, but that you can scratch, move and play with. Documentary – lots of empty coffee cups while you work in a crew on a documentary project.

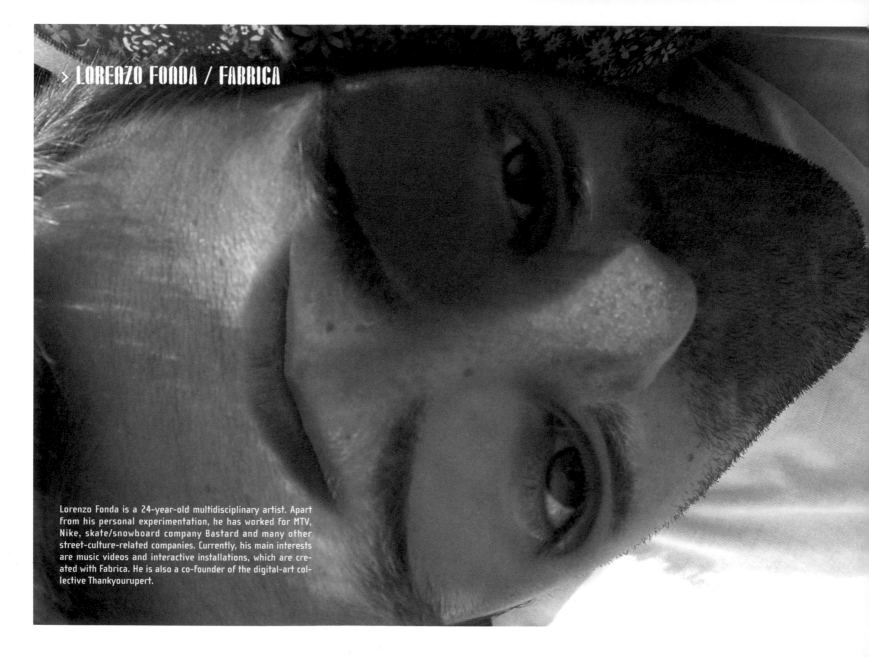

> LORENZO FONDA / FABRICA

Lorenzo Fonda is a 24-year-old multidisciplinary artist. Apart from his personal experimentation, he has worked for MTV, Nike, skate/snowboard company Bastard and many other street-culture-related companies. Currently, his main interests are music videos and interactive installations, which are created with Fabrica. He is also a co-founder of the digital-art collective Thankyourupert.

IdN: How did Fabrica get involved in the short-film field?

LF: When a student wants to create a personal short movie, Fabrica helps by financing and providing us with support, either "artistic" or logistical. They also help you with making your movie known to the outer world. Fabrica has always been involved with video and film, even since the beginning with Godfrey Reggio's exceptional vision.

IdN: If you ever had an approach from a major movie-maker, who would you most like to work with?

LF: I don't think I'm actually prepared to make movies, and there are too many directors I like. I would like to work with people who create funny and serious works at the same time. Maybe Spike Jonze, because of our same skateboarding background. I'd love to make a skate video with him. There are too many, really. If I created a story it would not reflect directly the reality of life: I'm more interested in the ways we can comment on human experience rather than trying to explain it.

IdN: Describe your favourite movie-viewing venue.

LF: I like to see films at the cinema. It makes for a more complete experience and heightens the dignity of a movie.

IdN: What is your favourite movie?

LF: You know, it's impossible to say. I just have memories of enlightening experiences. I remember Amarcord from Fellini, it was amazing. I love movies that are character-based. The 25th Hour by Spike Lee was the last film I saw that touched me deeply.

IdN: How would you define the differences between film and movie?

LF: There isn't any difference, they're the same things. Maybe there's a difference between video and film: the first allows you more experimentation and improvisation with images, the second makes for a more compelling experience, but it requires a lot of organisation and disclipine.

IdN: Where would you most like to have your work screened?

LF: For sure at the cinema, with a huge sound system and a big screen.

IdN: How do you feel about the growing popularity of the short-film genre?

LF: Competition is fine. I just feel fulfilled and inspired when I see someone's good work. People should both produce their shorts and be able to "market" them by themselves, in whatever category – independent filmmaking, mainstream movies, music videos, documentaries, etc. – they want to fit. On the other hand, I think a strong selection should be made, to create a higher level of top-quality products. Some institutions and events are doing that, and it's good.

HOUSE 1 : DRAMA
NIP/TUCK

> DIGITAL.KITCHEN

SEE ALSO :
> KINGDOM HOSPITAL 026   > SECONDHAND LIONS 106
> THE 6TH DAY 144

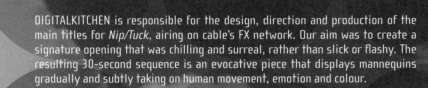

DIGITALKITCHEN is responsible for the design, direction and production of the main titles for *Nip/Tuck*, airing on cable's FX network. Our aim was to create a signature opening that was chilling and surreal, rather than slick or flashy. The resulting 30-second sequence is an evocative piece that displays mannequins gradually and subtly taking on human movement, emotion and colour.

> **Executive Creative Director:** Paul Matthaeus > **Creative Director:** Paul Schneider > **Associate Creative Director/Lead Designer:** Vince Haycock > **Flame/compositor:** Chris Markos > **Animators:** Vince Haycock, Chris Markos > **Executive Producer:** Don McNeill > **Producer:** Mark Bashore > **Editorial:** Eric Anderson > **Client:** FX Networks – Shepherd/Robin Co.

ANARCHISTS' CONVENTION PRESENTS

THORA BIRCH

CHRIS COOPER

CHRIS COOPER

TIM ROTH

RALPH WAITE

HOUSE 1 : DRAMA

SILVER CITY

> IMAGINARY FORCES

SEE ALSO :
> HELLBOY 134
> THE STEPFORD WIVES 066
> THE HITCHHIKER'S GUIDE TO THE GALAXY 148

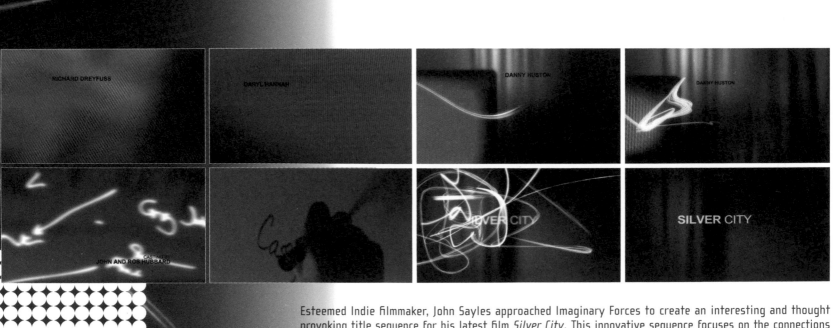

Esteemed Indie filmmaker, John Sayles approached Imaginary Forces to create an interesting and thought provoking title sequence for his latest film *Silver City*. This innovative sequence focuses on the connections between the people entwined in this movie's plot of political intrigue, scandal, and personal accountability. The inspiration for the title sequence originated from the main character's use of a marker on a wall to draw maps and make connections between the leads in the film as well as the case within it. IF created a 3D environment in which a CG felt-tip marker writes in space, connecting the text of the titles as if they were the names on the apartment wall of the main character.

> **Title:** *Silver City* > **Length:** 1:45 > **Date aired:** Spetember 17th, 2004 > **Description:** Main title sequence for independent film by John Sayles > **Designed & Produced by:** Imaginary Forces (IF) / Art Director(s): Ahmet Ahmet / Designers: Ahmet Ahmet, Charles Khoury / Head of Production: Chip Houghton / Producer: Greg Talmage / Editor: Danielle White / Inferno Artist: Rod Basham / 3D Animator(s): Charles Khoury, Sean Koriakin / Coordinator(s): Troy Miller / Sound Desinger: Danielle White > **Studio:** Director: John Sayles / Exec. Producer(s): Maggie Renzi / Producer(s): Maggie Renzi / Post Production Supervisor: Kendall McCarthyEditor: Plummy Tucker, John Sayles

> IMAGINARY FORCES

Imaginarg Forces is an entertainment, design, and production agency base in Hollywood and New York City. Their award-winning work spans the diverse industries of commercial advertising, branding, feature production and marketing, archtecture, sports, and interactive media. IF's work includes main title sequences for *Hellboy, Spider-man, The Cat in the Hat and Seven*. Upcoming title sequences in *Ray, and Blade: Trinity*. Additionally, IF has created teaser/trailers for such films as *The Stepford Wives, Men in Black I and II and Signs*; television main title sequences for Touching Evil, NASCAR Drivers: 360, Karen Sisco and Band of Brothers. IF has produced network packages for Animal Planet, The Discovery Channel, Lifetime and MTV; acclaimed commercial campaigns for Outdoor Life Network, Crest, Dove, Nike, and Sears. Fusing archtecture and media, IF has created branded experiences for Morgan Stanley, IBM, and the NFL's Baltimore Ravens, Curretnly, IF is in post-production on its third film, *Blade: Trinity*, out in December 2004.

IdN: Your company's name is called "Imaginary Forces", what is your force of imaginary?

IF: The name comes from the prologue of Shakespeare's *Henry V*, in which the audience is asked to imagine the stage before them as a grand historical setting filled with dramatic events. We're blessed (and cursed!) with over-active imaginations that we channel into stories and environments. My favorite imaginary force? Probably surprise.

IdN: Knowing that besides making film title, making TV main titles is also one of your skills. Are there any big differences in terms of production and nature of making title for these two different media?

IF: When designing a main title for a feature film, you work on creating a sequence that appears at a very specific point within the narrative. For television, you have to consider that the main title might be seen many times, if the show is a series. The tv title may also have to function as an introduction to the recurring cast, or need to introduce the show to both a returning and new audience weekly. But for both film and tv the goal is the same — to make something specific to the show's themes and storyline — something both visually and conceptually expressive.

IdN: What would be the fun part making an opening title?

IF: Conceptualizing it, writing ideas, designing it and making storyboards, shooting it, editing it, finding music, figuring out animation, brainstorming, collaborating with the director, checking the film (it's like a little coloured jewel, when seen through a magnifying loop on a lightbox) , seeing it projected (still magical!)...all these parts of the process can be fun. Working from concept to finish is really satisfying. I'd have to say one of my favourite parts is in the beginning, brainstorming, and there's that wonderful sense of possibility as you dive into the film's world to come up with ideas.

IdN: Describe your most favourite movie-viewing place.

IF: I love old movie palaces, big grand theatrical spaces that haven't been chopped up. In LA, Mann's Chinese is a favourite, as is the Vista. Oh, and the Cineramadome down the street...

IdN: What is your favourite movie?

IF: Too many to mention ...but some favorites include *Rear Window*, *In the Mood for Love*, *The Usual Suspects*, *Rushmore*, *Grease*, *The Yellow Submarine*, Pixar animated films...

IdN: How would you define the differences between film and movie?

IF: I don't really see the difference...

IdN: How and where would be your favourite place for your works?

IF: To be shown? On a big screen with an advanced sound system turned up, maybe at one of those movie palaces!

IdN: The popularity of short film is getting higher and higher, more and more competitions of short films are being run. As a creator of short film, how you feel about that? From your point of view what would be the most effective and useful way allow more and more short film exposure?

IF: It's fantastic that short films that don't fit into traditional categories are getting more popular-work that mixes things up and can't be neatly defined. It's great that more festivals recognize this, because it's inspiring to both screen and view things with an audience, and also to be creating within a community. I like that the inclusion of DVDs with magazines and books is allowing for more distribution as well. I'd say the combination of these festivals and publications with a web presence allows for more useful film exposure. We head online to both browse and look up pieces we've heard about — the web allows us to share quickly too, always a plus.

HOUSE 1 : DRAMA
SKATIN'

> GREGORY BRUNKALLA

SEE ALSO :
> CELLPHONES 012   > MURALS 102
> STRANGLER 054

These roller skaters gather every weekend in Central Park to skate and dance. I originally went to Central Park with my friend Luke to shoot something completely different, but then we saw these roller skaters and we just had to use them. They are dancing to whatever music the DJ was playing, but I took that out in post and added tracks by Chromeo (Vice Records).

> **Direction by:** G.Brunkalla > **Camera by:** Luke McCoubrey

HOUSE 1 : DRAMA
SPYGAME

> YU+CO.

There was a time when CIA operative Nathan Muir and his protégé Tom Bishop were insepa-rable, travelling the world and tasting everything it had to offer ... from Vietnam to Berlin to Beirut. In a profession fraught with danger and uncertainty, Muir and Bishop forged an uncommonly close friendship based on mutual respect and affection. But that was years ago. Now, on the brink of his retirement from the agency, Muir learns that Bishop has gone rogue. His one-time protégé has been jailed in Beijing on espionage charges after attempting to break a prisoner out of China. Years of bad blood and hurt feelings are washed away in a flood of memories of adventures shared by the two men as Muir takes on his most dangerous – and personal – mission ever.

> **Creative director:** Garson Yu > **Producer:** Tim Thompson > **Designers/animators:** Benjamin Cuenod and Wayland Vida > **Inferno artist:** Todd Mesher > **Client:** Tony Scott > **Director:** Universal Pictures, studio.

HOUSE 1 : DRAMA
STRANGLER

> GREGORY BRUNKALLA

SEE ALSO :
> CELLPHONES 012
> SHATIN' 050
> MURALS 102

A music video for Calla (Arena Rock). This is the first music video that I worked on. It was shot in my apartment in Brooklyn for $0 so it was thanks to my job with Outpost Digital that we were able to hook it up with post. This is not a green-screen compositing effect as some people might think, but we just attached these small panel backdrops to a rig that attached to the camera. So the band members just stayed in place while we moved all around them. It gives a great floating effect and it's super inexpensive. Created with Adam Wills, Mark Mahaney and J. Penry.

> **Music by:** Calla > **Label by:** Arena Rock > **Director:** Gregory Brunkalla > **Production:** Adam Wills, Mark Mahaney, J. Penry

HOUSE 1 : DRAMA
TAKING LIVES

> 4U+CO.

SEE ALSO :
> CATWOMAN 124
> SPYGAME 052
> THE LAST SHOT 062
> WICKER PARK 078

> IMAGINING ARGENTINA 022
> THE CHRONICLES OF RIDDICK 146
> THE RECRUIT 064

A top FBI profiler, Special Agent Illeana Scott doesn't rely on traditional crime-solving techniques to unravel the mysteries of a murderous mind. Her intuitive, unconventional approach often makes the crucial difference between catching a killer and sending a dead-end case to the cold file. When Montreal detectives, handling a local homicide investigation, reluctantly ask for an outsider's help to get inside the head of a cunning serial killer, Agent Scott joins the case. With meticulous insight, she theorises that the chameleon-like killer is "life-jacking" – assuming the lives and identities of his victims. As the pressure mounts to catch the elusive murderer, Agent Scott's unorthodox methods alienate her from a territorial police team that feels threatened by her uncanny abilities. Her seemingly cold demeanour belies an unparalleled passion for her work, and she's at her best when she's working alone. However, when an unexpected attraction sparks a complicated romantic entanglement, the consummate specialist begins to doubt her finely honed instincts. Alone in an unfamiliar city with no-one she can trust, Agent Scott suddenly finds herself on a twisted and terrifying journey, surrounded by suspects in a case that has become chillingly personal.

> **Director/creative director:** Garson Yu > **Producer:** Buzz Hays > **Art director:** Yolanda Santosa > **Editor:** Joel Plotch > **Inferno artist:** Danny Mudgett > **D.P.:** Kramer Morgenthau > **Client:** D.J. Caruso > **Director:** Warner Bros., studio.

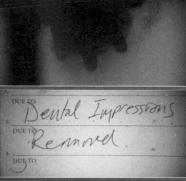

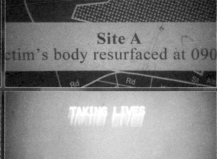

The unexpected world of Japanese horror with a sequence steeped in blood and fear for director Takashi Shimizu's American debut, *The Grudge*.

The sequence features a bottomless pool of translucent red liquid that has long strands of black hair undulating through. A single child's hand strikes the surface from below, and motivates the ripples for the title to reveal. The titles themselves are made from ripples and ink that flows in the bloody water.

> **Creative Director:** William Lebeda > **Art Director:** Elaine Alderette > **Producer:** Christina Hwang > **Designers:** Elaine Alderette, Akemi Abe, Jon Block > **Lead Compostitor:** Josh Novak > **3D Animator:** Jon Block > **2D Animators:** Akemi Abe, Nelson Yu, Josh Novak

HOUSE 1 : DRAMA
THE GRUDGE

> PICTURE MILL

SEE ALSO :
> I, ROBOT 136

Picture Mill located in California US, with a mission to find innovative and appropriate methods for communication. Putting a solid, significant idea together, find the form that best communicates that idea, and check it regularly for appropriateness. Never had a 'look' that defines the company's design in general. Picture Mill believe this could free them from being forced to repeat design solutions that were only appropriate for previous work.

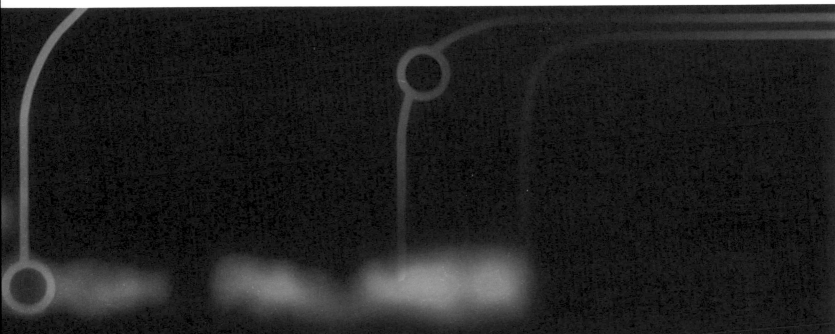

IdN: People tend to over look/misconception toward trailer/opening title, not knowing professional company does trailer and opening title. How would you feel about that?

PM: The work is usually its own reward, but it is nice when our titles are noticed and mentioned along with the films and their actors and directors. It doesn't bother us that most people don't know about title companies... we're a very small group in Hollywood. Though it is sometimes hard to explain to our friends and parents, outside of the film industry, exactly what we do and how we do it.

IdN: Your company is so well known for making opening titles, is there any of your previous works memorable, why is it so memorable? Would it because there were some difficulties while making it?

PM: Some of our most memorable and successful sequences have been for *Panic Room*, *2Fast 2Furious*, and *I, Robot*. And now *The Grudge*. They are successes because they are all perfectly suited for the films, and add to the overall film experience, as well as stand alone as excellent examples of title design. I think the ease or difficulty in creating the work is quickly forgotten when the results are exceptional.

IdN: What would be the fun part in making an opening title?

PM: The personal interaction with the director and editor is always exciting, because you are a direct part of the filmmaking process. But the best two moments of film title design are the beginning, when a project starts, with renewed excitement and ideas flowing, and the end, seeing the final piece completed, and integrated into the finished film.

IdN: What could be the most difficult part of making an opening title?

PM: Actually making it. Ideas are easy, but bringing them to life is hard...

IdN: Describe your most favourite movie-viewing place.

PM: The Historic Cinerama Dome, in the heart Hollywood.

IdN: What is your favourite movie?

PM: *True stories, After Hours, Jaws, Star Wars, Raiders of the Lost Arc, The Magnificent Seven, Fight Club, Cinema Paradiso, Full Metal Jacket*. And too many others to list here.

IdN: How would you define the differences between film and movie?

PM: A film is what leaves the editing room. A movie is what arrives at the theater.

IdN: How and where would be your favorite place for your works screening?

PM: In a theatre, with a box of popcorn.

THE LAST SHOT

> YU+CO.

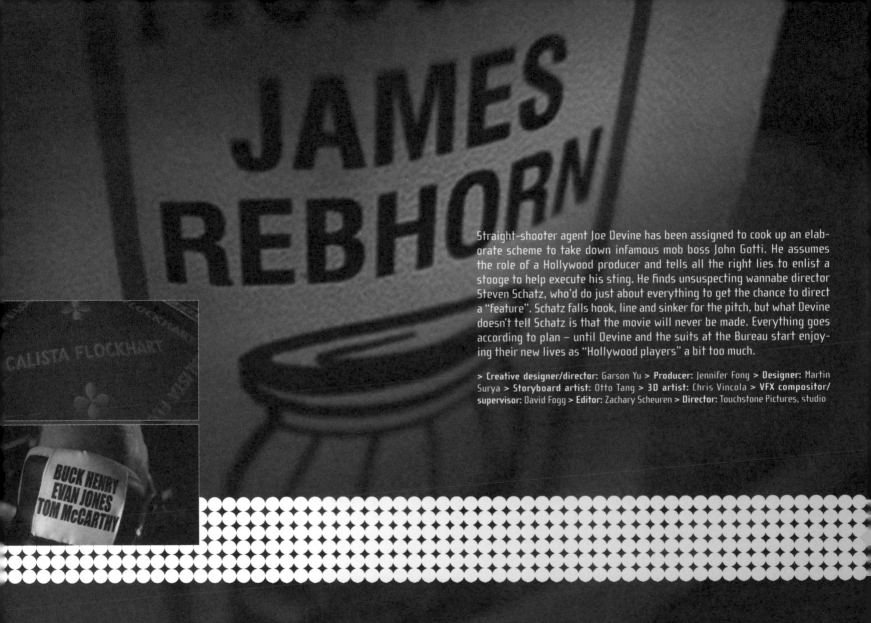

JAMES
REBHORN

CALISTA FLOCKHART

BUCK HENRY
EVAN JONES
TOM McCARTHY

Straight-shooter agent Joe Devine has been assigned to cook up an elaborate scheme to take down infamous mob boss John Gotti. He assumes the role of a Hollywood producer and tells all the right lies to enlist a stooge to help execute his sting. He finds unsuspecting wannabe director Steven Schatz, who'd do just about everything to get the chance to direct a "feature". Schatz falls hook, line and sinker for the pitch, but what Devine doesn't tell Schatz is that the movie will never be made. Everything goes according to plan – until Devine and the suits at the Bureau start enjoying their new lives as "Hollywood players" a bit too much.

> **Creative designer/director:** Garson Yu > **Producer:** Jennifer Fong > **Designer:** Martin Surya > **Storyboard artist:** Otto Tang > **3D artist:** Chris Vincola > **VFX compositor/supervisor:** David Fogg > **Editor:** Zachary Scheuren > **Director:** Touchstone Pictures, studio

HOUSE 1 : DRAMA
THE RECRUIT

> 4U+CO.

E RECRUIT

James Clayton might not have the attitude of a typical recruit, but he is one of the smartest graduating seniors in the country – and he's just the person that Walter Burke wants in the Agency. James regards the CIA's mission as an intriguing alternative to an ordinary life, but before he becomes an Ops Officer, James has to survive The Farm, where the veteran Burke teaches him the ropes and rules of the game. James quickly rises through the ranks and falls for Layla, one of his fellow recruits. But just when James starts to question his role and decides to "wash out", Burke taps him for a special assignment to root out a mole. It soon becomes clear that at The Farm, the CIA's old maxims are true: "Trust no one" and "Nothing is as it seems."

> **Designer/Creative Director:** Garson Yu > **Executive Producer:** Jennifer Fong > **Designer:** Martin Surya > **Animator:** Wayland Vida > **Inferno Artist:** Todd Mesher > **Client:** Roger Donaldson > **Director:** Touchstone Pictures, studio.

THE STEPFORD WIVES

> IMAGINARY FORCES

SEE ALSO :
> HELLBOY 134
> THE HITCHHIKER'S GUIDE TO THE GALAXY 148

> SILVER CITY 046

Based on the idea that you can have the perfect life, the teaser/trailer for *The Stepford Wives* showcases all of the most amazing products ... all of the best things that you can buy and have made "just for you." Playing with the ideas of excessive consumerism and the Stepford male fantasy of creating the ideal spouse, in the end we reveal Nicole Kidman as the ultimate product herself, a Stepford Wife.

> **Title:** *The Stepford Wives* > **Description:** Teaser Trailer > **Designed & Produced by:** Imaginary Forces [IF] / Creative Director: Peter Frankfurt / Director / Art Director: Sara Marandi / Director of Photography: Harris Savides / Designers: Sara Marandi, Karin Fong, Peggy Oei / 2D Animators: Vinnie Fugre, Charles Khoury / Copywriters: Peter Frankfurt, Anita Olan, Paul Rudnick / Head of Production / Producer: Anita Olan / Associate Producers: Ben Apley, Joanna Fillie / Live Action Producers: Maureen Ryan, Kira Dixon > **Studio:** Paramount Pictures / Executive Vice-President, Marketing/Creative Affairs: Nancy Goliger / Editorial Company: Giaronomo / Editor: Adam Agard / Producers: Ron Auerbach, Giacomo Vieste

RYTHING YOU OWN IS BEAUTIFUL

THE STEPFORD WIVES

HOUSE 1 : DRAMA
TRIP

> NE-0

A short narrative involving a chain reaction of events that accidentally links strangers together.

> **Director:** NE-O > **Music:** Rashad Omer > **Producer:** Richard Fenton > **Production Manager:** Noreen Khan > **DOP:** Richard Stewart > **Editing, Post Production:** EYECANDY > **Cast:** Delivery Guy: Rupert Blanchard / Office Lady: Simone Bowkett / Jogger: Steven Murray / Skater: Charlie Young > Thanks to: Academy, Black Island Studios, Take 2, Direct Lighting, Lawrence & CO, Twingo

> NE-O

Blending live-action, animation and graphics, NE-O creates a new format of motion-image for idents, promos, and commercials with a strong focus on dark humour and spatial-temporal visual tricks.

Working as a directing duo since the beginning of 2002, Jake Knight and Ryoko Tanaka are NE-O the new directing team from postproduction company Eyecandy. It was Jake's short film Salaryman 6 shot for onedotzero6 and written by Ryoko, that went on to win "best short film" at the Rushes Soho shorts festival 2002, and 2nd Prize in TCM Classic Shorts award 2002 in London Film Festival that really got people talking about their talent.

Since then, they have been working on commercials for Coca Cola, Sonyericsson, VW and Music videos for Blackstrobe, Futureshock and Ken Ishii. The music video for Futureshock Late at Night has just awarded the 2004 CADS award for Best Special Effects of the music video, and nominated for Best Dance Video.

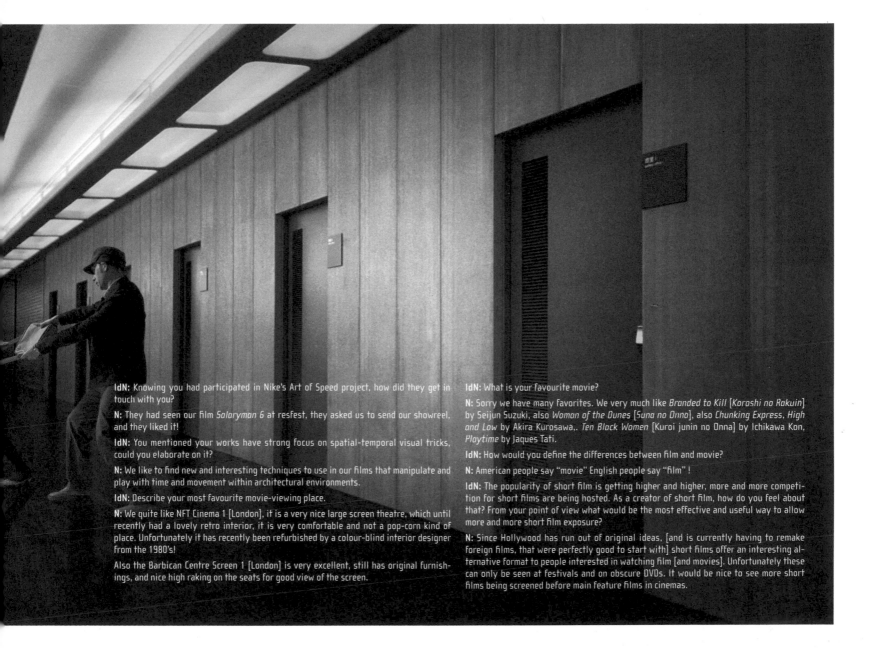

IdN: Knowing you had participated in Nike's Art of Speed project, how did they get in touch with you?

N: They had seen our film *Salaryman 6* at resfest, they asked us to send our showreel, and they liked it!

IdN: You mentioned your works have strong focus on spatial-temporal visual tricks, could you elaborate on it?

N: We like to find new and interesting techniques to use in our films that manipulate and play with time and movement within architectural environments.

IdN: Describe your most favourite movie-viewing place.

N: We quite like NFT Cinema 1 [London], it is a very nice large screen theatre, which until recently had a lovely retro interior, it is very comfortable and not a pop-corn kind of place. Unfortunately it has recently been refurbished by a colour-blind interior designer from the 1980's!

Also the Barbican Centre Screen 1 [London] is very excellent, still has original furnishings, and nice high raking on the seats for good view of the screen.

IdN: What is your favourite movie?

N: Sorry we have many favorites. We very much like *Branded to Kill* [*Koroshi no Rakuin*] by Seijun Suzuki, also *Woman of the Dunes* [*Suna no Onna*], also *Chunking Express*, *High and Low* by Akira Kurosawa,. *Ten Black Women* [Kuroi junin no Onna] by Ichikawa Kon, *Playtime* by Jaques Tati.

IdN: How would you define the differences between film and movie?

N: American people say "movie" English people say "film" !

IdN: The popularity of short film is getting higher and higher, more and more competition for short films are being hosted. As a creator of short film, how do you feel about that? From your point of view what would be the most effective and useful way to allow more and more short film exposure?

N: Since Hollywood has run out of original ideas, [and is currently having to remake foreign films, that were perfectly good to start with] short films offer an interesting alternative format to people interested in watching film [and movies]. Unfortunately these can only be seen at festivals and on obscure DVDs. It would be nice to see more short films being screened before main feature films in cinemas.

HOUSE 1 : DRAMA
VANITY FAIR

> TROLLBÄCK+COMPANY

SEE ALSO :
> NIKE BUTTERFLY 104

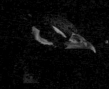

a Mira Nair film

Reese Witherspoon

VANITY *fair*

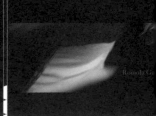

Gabriel Byrne

Ronnie G

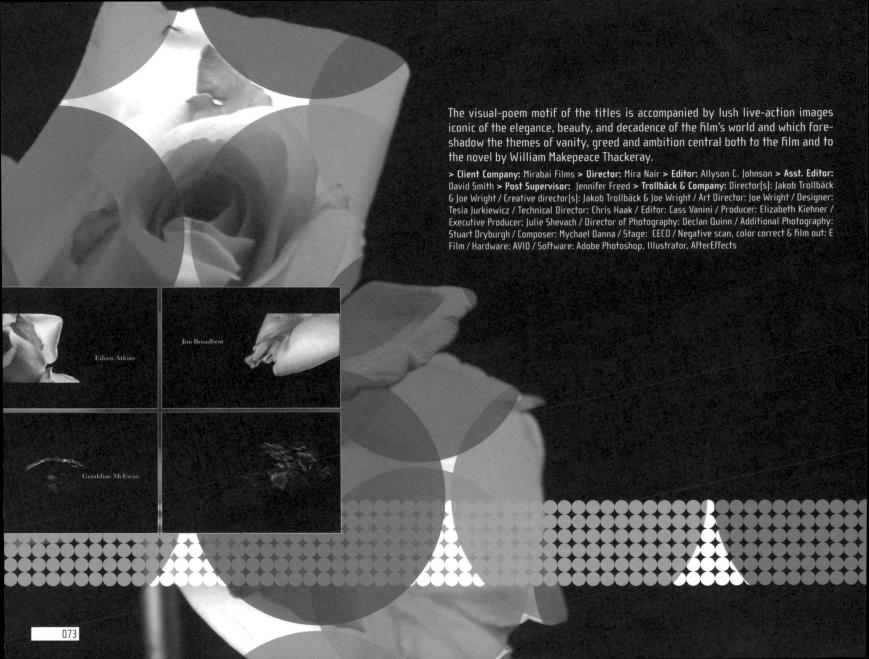

The visual-poem motif of the titles is accompanied by lush live-action images iconic of the elegance, beauty, and decadence of the film's world and which foreshadow the themes of vanity, greed and ambition central both to the film and to the novel by William Makepeace Thackeray.

> **Client Company:** Mirabai Films > **Director:** Mira Nair > **Editor:** Allyson C. Johnson > **Asst. Editor:** David Smith > **Post Supervisor:** Jennifer Freed > **Trollbäck & Company:** Director(s): Jakob Trollbäck & Joe Wright / Creative director(s): Jakob Trollbäck & Joe Wright / Art Director: Joe Wright / Designer: Tesia Jurkiewicz / Technical Director: Chris Haak / Editor: Cass Vanini / Producer: Elizabeth Kiehner / Executive Producer: Julie Shevach / Director of Photography: Declan Quinn / Additional Photography: Stuart Dryburgh / Composer: Mychael Danna / Stage: CECO / Negative scan, color correct & film out: E Film / Hardware: AVID / Software: Adobe Photoshop, Illustrator, AfterEffects

Eileen Atkins

Jim Broadbent

Geraldine McEwan

Full spread: *Vanity Fair*'s behind scene

> TROLLBÄCK+COMPANY

According to Trollbäck & Company's CEO and creative director Jakob Trollbäck: "The key to good design is staying invigorated, taking what you know and applying it to new areas so that, as a company and as individuals, you can grow creatively." And it is precisely this commitment to new influences that fuels the company's diverse creative output: commercials, film titles, environmental installations and network TV branding all fall under Trollbäck's creative umbrella.

Known throughout the television, film and design industries for its clean, aesthetic and avant-garde approach, the three-year-old firm has rapidly risen to prominence through little more than word-of-mouth. Generating the buzz is an eclectic mix of design projects for top-shelf clients such as HBO, TNT, AMC, Sundance Channel, Volvo and Sony, as well as successful forays into short films, snowboard graphics and T-shirts.

IdN: Making TV main titles is one of your areas of expertise. Are there any big differences in terms of production between this and short-movie-making?

JT: When designing and producing main titles for TV, you clearly have less time than for a typical short-film production, and are given someone else's idea, usually from a network or agency. Often with a short film, the director is also the writer, so he/she has more creative freedom. This does not mean, however, that working with boundaries and restrictions is always a negative.

IdN: Do you think MTV could also be considered as short film?

JT: Yes, I believe music videos can be considered short films. Even though music videos are vehicles to promote a band or an artist and create hype, some still have the ability to tell a story. It's not so much about visually promoting the band members as creating a unique visual/narrative that will get people talking. A lot of times today, the artist/band members are not even featured in the video.

IdN: What is the fun part making an opening title?

JT: Well, working closely with the feature-film's director is great. Often title sequences stand alone – acting as a two to three-minute prologue to a movie. It gives us a chance to be narrative and set the atmosphere for the movie before the first scene.

IdN: Describe your favourite movie-viewing venue.

JT: The Ritzy Cinema in Brixton, England. Originally built in 1910 as the Electric Pavilion, The Ritzy is an independent, local London cinema showing an eclectic bunch of art-house, independent, mainstream and world films.

IdN: What is your favourite movie?

JT: I have many, but right now I'll say *Chungking Express* by Wong Kar-Wai.

IdN: How would you define the differences between film and movie?

JT: I'm from England, so it's film!

IdN: Where would you most like to see your work screened?

JT: Times Square. Or projected on the Hollywood sign also would be interesting.

IdN: How do you feel about the growing popularity of short film and the increasing number of festivals and competitions devoted to it?

JT: Competition is good. How many people are creating films doesn't matter because you will still only have a handful of really, really good ones. Technology has changed so that now anyone with a camera and an idea can go out and shoot. Editing can easily be accomplished on a Mac. A short film is about the concept, the idea, and not so much about the production value.

HOUSE 1 : DRAMA
WICKER PARK

> 4U+CO.

WICKE

METRO-GOLDWYN-MAYER PICTURES AND LAKESHORE ENTERTAINMENT PRESENT

A LAKESHORE ENTERTAINMENT PRODUCTION

JOSH HARTNETT

From the moment Matthew sees Lisa, nothing else matters. She walks past the window of the shop where he works in the Wicker Park section of Chicago, and he's immediately captivated; he follows her, they meet, and soon they fall deeply in love. Everything about their relationship seems perfect – until the day she disappears without a trace. Two years later, Matt has built a new life for himself, but he's still haunted by her memory and the nagging torment of unanswered questions. Then he catches a quick glimpse of someone he thinks must be her in a bar – but is it? Thus begins a twisting, obsessive search for the woman who captured his heart years ago – and for someone who's playing with his mind right now. Matthew's search for the truth will lead him deeper into the mystery, with each discovery more deceiving than the next. Obsession can go both ways, and Matthew discovers it's possible to love someone too much.

> **Creative director:** Garson Yu > **Executive producer:** Jennifer Fong > **Editor:** Tony Fulgham > **Typographer:** Yolanda Santosa > **Client:** Paul McGuigan > **Director:** MGM Pictures, studio.

PARK

WICKE

WICKER PARK

PRODUCED BY
TOM ROSENBERG
GARY LUCCHESI

HOUSE 2 : FANTASY

There is a thin line between sci-fi and fantasy and people tend to mix them up. Essentially, the world
that is created in a sci-fi movie, no matter how advanced or even unbelievable the technology depicted,
could actually happen in real life, albeit far into the future. Fantasy, on the other hand, is mostly based
on myth and urban legend, through humanised forms such as elves and representations of good and evil,
with gods who express anger or pleasure towards the real world. Fantasy films often involve a battle
between the forces of human nature and Mother Nature and are invariably inspirational
in terms of showing characters striving to achieve a dream or a goal.

HOUSE 2 : FANTASY
A GHOST IN FABRICA

> LORENZO FONDA / FABRICA

SEE ALSO :
> NIKE : OLE 036

A young ghost flies around Fabrica for his two weeks trial period, but no one notices him.

> **Director and photography:** Lorenzo Fonda > www.cerberoleso.it > **Music:** written by bernhard fleischmann (www.bfleischmann.com) > Taken from the album *welcome tourist* on morr music (www.morrmusic.com) > **Published by:** m+s industries/neue welt musikverlag

FIZZY EYE

> NEXUS PRODUCTIONS LTD

SEE ALSO :
> CATCH ME IF YOU CAN 008   > MIRANDA 034
> THUNDERBIRDS 160

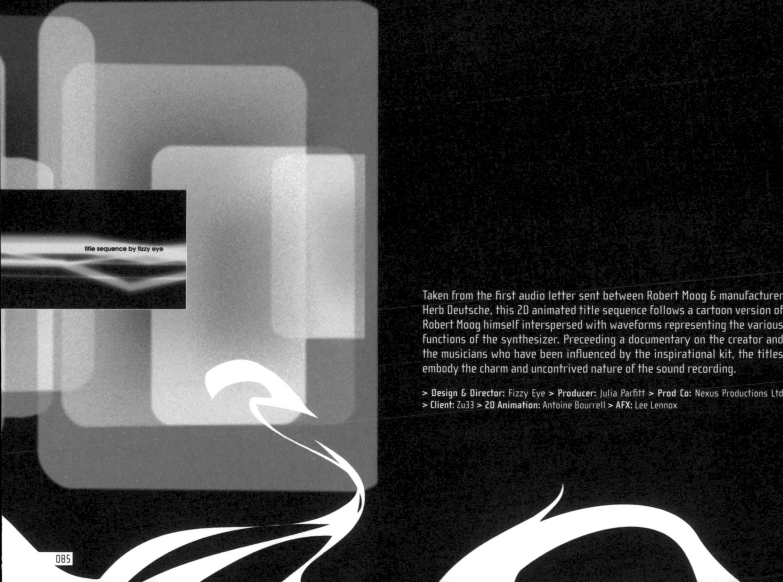

title sequence by fizzy eye

Taken from the first audio letter sent between Robert Moog & manufacturer
Herb Deutsche, this 2D animated title sequence follows a cartoon version of
Robert Moog himself interspersed with waveforms representing the various
functions of the synthesizer. Preceeding a documentary on the creator and
the musicians who have been influenced by the inspirational kit, the titles
embody the charm and uncontrived nature of the sound recording.

> **Design & Director:** Fizzy Eye > **Producer:** Julia Parfitt > **Prod Co:** Nexus Productions Ltd
> **Client:** Zu33 > **2D Animation:** Antoine Bourrell > **AFX:** Lee Lennox

HOUSE 2 : FANTASY
I'M FALLING FOREVER

> HONEST

SEE ALSO :
> FASTER WAY TO START THE DAY 204

FALLING MAN

SIGHTINGS

For Diesel's "Dream Maker" campaign, they asked 30 artists and directors to create a one-minute movie of a dream from one of the characters from the print ads. Ours, titled *Falling Man*, follows a man as he falls from a ladder while trying to change a light bulb — when he hits the ground he bursts through the floor and keeps on falling through other people's apartments, restaurants, offices, museums, bathrooms, beaches, etc., until he starts to become a bit of a celebrity. It all comes to a screeching halt when he falls onto a trampoline.

> Directed by: HONEST **> Written by:** HONEST **> Cast:** Gregory Brunkalla – Falling Man / Paula Taylor – Wife / Richard Holland – Husband / Julie McNiven – Girlfriend / Gregory Murnion – Boyfriend / Theodore Bouloukos II – Hairy Man / Shawn Smith – Neighbor 1 / Neighbor 2 / Marc Blang – Office Worker / Marco Morillo – Chef 1 / Debbie Lyn – Chef 2 / John Freeman – Coffee Drinker / Michele Gramesty – Woman on Beach / Christian Lynch – Newspaper Man / Michael Barnard – Puzzle Player / Alex Greene – TV Watcher / Michael Brooks – Weather Man / Chiara Alberetti – Woman in Train / Roanne Adams – Woman in Museum / Jim Coppola – Man in Field 1 / John Coppola – Man in Field 2 / Janet Coppola – Woman in Field 1 / Michele Gramesty – Woman in Field 2 / Chiara Alberetti – Woman in Field 3 **> Produced by:** Producer – HONEST / Producer – Gregory Brunkalla / Executive Producer – Antoinnette Advento / Executive Producer – Chiara Alberetti / Executive Producer – Jim Coppola / Executive Producer – Jason Lynn **> Edited by:** HONEST **> Sound Design by:** Eric Offin **> Original Music by:** Mark Garcia **> Cinematography by:** HONEST, Gregory Brunkalla **> Post Production by:** Outpost Digital **> Special Effects by:** Outpost Digital **> Casting by:** HONEST **> Production Management:** HONEST **> Production Assistants:** Jesse James, Jonathan Jackson, Jose Ayala, John Freeman

Full spread: *I'm Falling Forever's* story board.

> HONEST

Founded in the Spring of 1997 by Jonathan Milott and Cary Murnion, who met while attending Parsons School of Design in New York, Honest is involved in a variety of projects including producing and directing films; editing and designing their own magazine called *Honest*; designing books, motion graphics and identities for a wide range of clients; teaching advanced broadcast design at Parsons; and showing art in various galleries around the world.

Recent projects include short films for Nike's "Art Of Speed" and Diesel's "Dream Maker" campaigns; show packages for Nickelodeon; a website for Magic Hat, a Vermont micro-brewery; and the re-branding of the New Museum of Contemporary Art, including identity work, the museum's website and its first formal advertising campaign.

Honest was recently selected by the Art Directors' Club to be a part of its Young Guns 4 exhibition and the company was featured at last year's International Design Conference in Aspen, chaired by Paola Antonelli, Design Curator for MoMA, addressing the topic "Safe: Design Takes On Risk". The work of Honest has been featured in *RES*, *The Fader*, *EYE*, *NYLON*, *Anthem*, *Creative Review*, *Print*, *STEP* and other magazines.

IdN: How did you come to participate in Nike's "Art Of Speed" and Diesel's "Dream Maker" projects?

Honest: Both Nike and Diesel contacted us because they liked our work and thought we'd bring something unique and inspiring to their film projects.

IdN: Besides making films, Honest also has its own magazine; is there any connection between the two?

Honest: The only connection is that the films and the magazine are made by the same people. I'm sure that we infuse are own personalities into both, but any direct links are not premeditated.

IdN: Describe your favourite movie-viewing venue.

Honest: The Ziegfeld Theater in New York City.

IdN: What is your favourite movie?

Honest: I don't have one favourite movie of all time, that would be too hard, but one that I watched again recently and was reminded of how much I love it was *Cool Hand Luke*. A more current movie that blew my socks off was *Triplettes Of Belleville*. And one of my favourite documentaries is *American Movie*.

IdN: How would you define the differences between film and movie?

Honest: I don't, really.

IdN: Where would be your favourite place for your works' screening?

Honest: The Ziegfeld Theater in New York City.

IdN: The popularity of short films is growing, and more and more short-film competitions are being hosted. As a creator of short films, how you feel about this? From your point of view, what would be the most effective and useful way to create more exposure for short films?

Honest: It's great that there are more avenues for filmmakers to get their work seen. The quality of the work will determine whether or not people stay interested in viewing these short films. So far I'd say it's about 50:50, so hopefully more and more directors will be inspired to make new, innovative work. The thing that will allow more short films to be exposed is higher bandwidth – and more corporate clients who realise the benefit of funding innovative art/film programmes.

IdN: If you could use a specific item to represent the following categorie – drama, fantasy, sci-fi, experimental and documentary – what would you choose?

Honest: Drama – Optimus Prime. Fantasy – W.M.D. Sci-fi – a mushroom. Experimental – a zipper. Documentary – a negligée.

HOUSE 2 : FANTASY

ITSU

> PLEIX

SEE ALSO :
> SOMETIMES 108

In the continuity of Beauty Kit, and always in a humorous way, this work constitutes a kind of parable of our consumer society and its hysteria. Pleix adopts a visual language that plays on limits, ambiguity and paradox that blurs the relationship with reality and provokes a strange unease. Music by Plaid on Warp records.

> Directed by: PLEIX > Music by: PLAID (Warp records) > Produced by: PLEIX.

> PLEIX

Pleix is a community of digital artists (graphic designers, 3D artists, directors, a musician, an editor and a project manager) willing to mix their skills to gain greater freedom for various projects. The collective was created in 2001. It consists of seven people, all based in Paris. But they never put their invidual names on anything, simply signing their different projects "Pleix". They say: "We are all complementary technically and creatively and it's an ideal situation for us to be together."

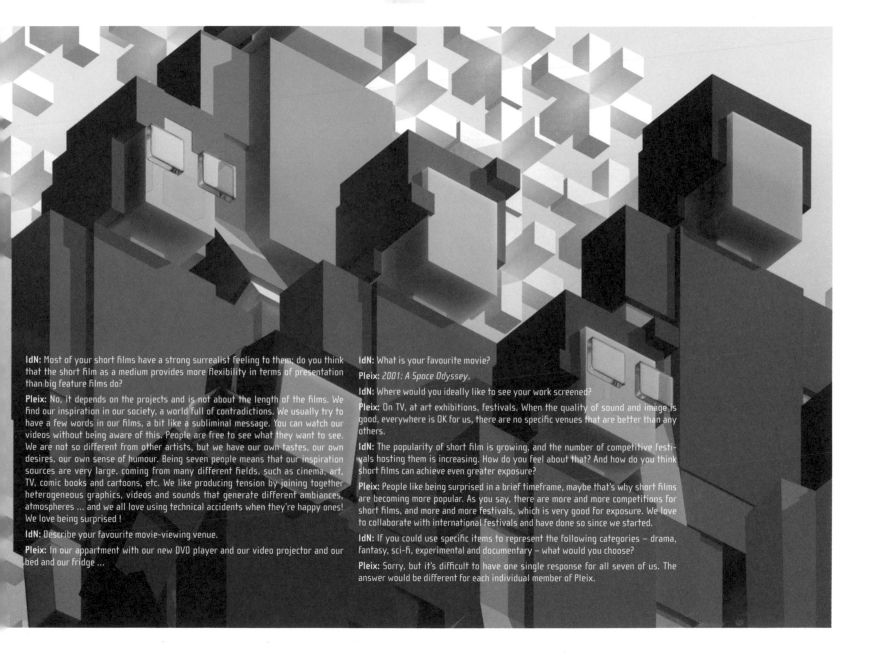

IdN: Most of your short films have a strong surrealist feeling to them: do you think that the short film as a medium provides more flexibility in terms of presentation than big feature films do?

Pleix: No, it depends on the projects and is not about the length of the films. We find our inspiration in our society, a world full of contradictions. We usually try to have a few words in our films, a bit like a subliminal message. You can watch our videos without being aware of this. People are free to see what they want to see. We are not so different from other artists, but we have our own tastes, our own desires, our own sense of humour. Being seven people means that our inspiration sources are very large, coming from many different fields, such as cinema, art, TV, comic books and cartoons, etc. We like producing tension by joining together heterogeneous graphics, videos and sounds that generate different ambiances, atmospheres ... and we all love using technical accidents when they're happy ones! We love being surprised !

IdN: Describe your favourite movie-viewing venue.

Pleix: In our appartment with our new DVD player and our video projector and our bed and our fridge ...

IdN: What is your favourite movie?

Pleix: *2001: A Space Odyssey*.

IdN: Where would you ideally like to see your work screened?

Pleix: On TV, at art exhibitions, festivals. When the quality of sound and image is good, everywhere is OK for us, there are no specific venues that are better than any others.

IdN: The popularity of short film is growing, and the number of competitive festivals hosting them is increasing. How do you feel about that? And how do you think short films can achieve even greater exposure?

Pleix: People like being surprised in a brief timeframe, maybe that's why short films are becoming more popular. As you say, there are more and more competitions for short films, and more and more festivals, which is very good for exposure. We love to collaborate with international festivals and have done so since we started.

IdN: If you could use specific items to represent the following categories – drama, fantasy, sci-fi, experimental and documentary – what would you choose?

Pleix: Sorry, but it's difficult to have one single response for all seven of us. The answer would be different for each individual member of Pleix.

KKF

> GINTS APSITS

SEE ALSO :
> THE BONEDANCER 114

Desperate artist has generated huge idea (bulb). So he is desperately walking around carrying the idea in his hands. There is some link missing, to make the idea shine – it turns out to be a lamp high up on the ceiling. There is no way for him to reach the lamp. Some strong state-of-the-art is coming. (It's a bird-headed man with a sceptre for an eye and a head of a sheep in a boat for lungs.) Together, they examine the idea carefully and decide that it is "really good". They give their blessings with fire (foundation). Stairs grow out of the fire up to the ceiling, to the lamp. The artist screws it in. And now it shines for everybody. Everybody is happy.

> **Director:** Gints Apsits > **Art and motion design:** Gints Apsits > **Camera & stopmotion scenography:** Gints Apsits > **Production:** Gints Apsits > **Sound:** Kaspars Bindemanis > **Agency:** ZOOM! > **Creative director:** Eriks Stendzenieks > **Year:** 2003 Dec.

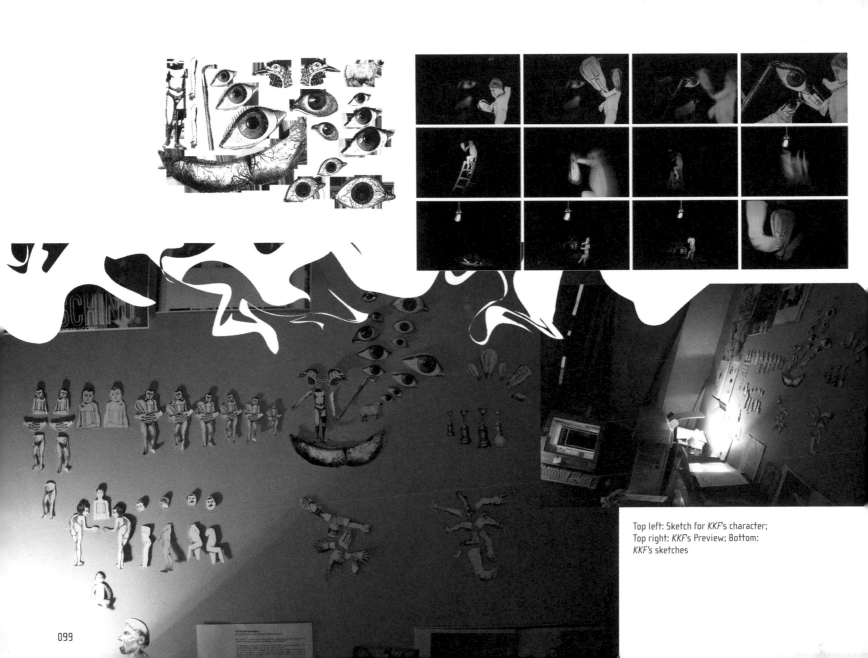

Top left: Sketch for *KKF*'s character;
Top right: *KKF*'s Preview; Bottom:
KKF's sketches

> GINTS APSITS

Besides working as an art director, illustrator and graphic designer, Gints has directed and animated international-award-winning commercials and short movies.

Based in Riga, Latvia, he freelances for local and international clients either through agencies, or directly with design and production studios.

After studying with Fabrica (Benetton's research and communication centre in Italy), he worked for clients such as Diesel, Killerloop, United Colors of Benetton, Kessels Kramer, DDB, McCann-Erickson and Colors. His work has been exhibited and screened around the world, including in Japan, the UK, Italy, Portugal, Germany, France and Norway.

www.apsits.com

IdN: Your work has a strong abstract feel to it; is this intentional, part of your style/identity?

Apsits: Yes. Because there is a lot of trendy stuff around such as vector motion, 3D and other FX or techniques that go along with certain software and trends. At some point you cease to be able to recognise the artist behind that. So I thought – why should I go the same way that everybody goes? It started with *The Bonedancer*. I was obsessed with making moving collage like bioform – pulsating, breathing, not just stiff and moving only in keypoints. It was in my head and I was totally sure I could do it. So I created *Bonedancer* in 2002. I'm not totally happy with it, it's still possible to recognise Liquify FX, for example, but I'll try to get rid of that in my next motion work.

All my stories and characters come out of surreal collage works. I have some 200 hand-made collages. So I sit down and think, what could be a story behind this? Why is this monkey sitting on this horse? Oh, perhaps it could represent dumb authority. Step by step it becomes a story. Lots of people have told me: "Great movie, but it lacks a story." Actually, there is a story behind it, but it's not so literal. When I tried to make the story more recognisable, as in *Girl Going For The Milk*, the movie became silly when those surreal characters started to act too literally.

I'm not necessarily going to stick with this style – I'm open, it's just a matter of time.

IdN: What triggers your passion for short-filmmaking?

Apsits: I'm envious of musicans, because no any other art form has touched me so deeply. Music grabs you so straight away and very strongly; it makes you cry or smile or jump out of the window during three to five minutes of a song. I never felt any graphic work so powerfully. I think I have solved this problem for myself by creating moving imagery to go along with song. So when I start to do some motion work I'm totally spellbound by the miracle that music can bring to it ... it's also fantastic to see how graphic motion gives power back to music.

IdN: Describe your favourite movie-viewing venue.

Apsits: Its really boring usually. When I am dead from working at the end of the day, I watch movies on my PC. Alone, with headphones, in the dark. I hate watching good movies with someone else.

IdN: What is your favourite movie?

Apsits: Works by Michel Gondry, Cunningham. Feature films by Jim Jarmush – *Stranger Then Paradise*, *Down By Law* ...

IdN: How would you define the differences between film and movies?

Apsits: I don't know much about the terminology, but I guess "movie" is a kind of general term for motion pictures, whereas film is movie shot on 35, 16 or 8mm, either transferred or screened from it. But I am not sure, never having been to film school or studied fat books on the subject.

IdN: Where would be your favourite place to screen your own works?

Apsits: In the year 1904, inside a huge whale cut in half, screened on its internal organs so that although the movie was in black-and-white it would be the first colour movie. Presented in the centre of London. An oldie club orchestra desperately trying to sync with the movie, based on the rhythms of the film, so some of them would drop dead with heart attacks.

IdN: The popularity of short film is growing and an increasing number of short-film festivals are being hosted. As a creator of short films, how you feel about this? What do you think is the most effective way of gaining more exposure for short films?

Apsits: They are quite suitable for Internet streaming. A lot of people have already recognised that and are working on it. It could be suitable for a new kind of cafeteria where there are 25-minute screenings every half-an-hour. So people can watch movies even during a break in the middle of the day. They could be screened in trains, metros, bus stations. Life becomes faster – so movies must become shorter. I think it's just a matter of time until companies realise the potency of a short over a feature.

IdN: If you could use a specific item to represent the following categories – drama, fantasy, sci-fi, experimental and documentary – what would you choose?

Apsits: For documentary I would use hidden cameras. So the main character would not know about his involvement (I'm working on one like this right now ... shhhh!). Experimental is when you dedicate a movie to figuring out how one specific technique works. For example, *Bonedancer* is dedicated to Liquify FX; there are no another animation techniques – just this. I never saw this particular FX dedicated to a whole movie before. Gondry has used Lego for a whole movie, someone else used a photocopier for each frame, someone used interactive story-telling, etc. So it depends; I have 30-40 scripts already written for such experiments.

HOUSE 2 : FANTASY
MURALS

> GREGORY BRUNKALLA

SEE ALSO :
> CELLPHONES 012
> STRANGLER 054

> SKATIN' 050

This was a project that was also created in my apartment. I just hung up some simple outdoor backgrounds and had artists perform in front of them.

After reviewing the footage, I realised that the most entertaining parts of the performances were when they messed up, so that's what I show. J. Penry, who draws the nudist family, was a great help on this project – he called up Miggy Littleton and Tara Jane O'Neil and Brad Shanks from the band Blood On The Wall.

> **Camera, sound by:** G. Brunkalla > **Cast:** Brad Shanks, J. Penry, Miggy Littleton, Tara Jane O'neil

Shox TL
(Defyum gravitus)

The Origin of the SP Series

NIKE BUTTERFLY

TROLLBÄCK+COMPANY

SEE ALSO :
> VANITY FAIR 072

The concept is based on looking at the two sides of the family tree (athletics and golf) as different species. When placed together, the shoes have a strong resemblance to butterflies, the patterns and textures creating a unique personality for each style. We open on the athletic side of the group. We represent the shoes like butterflies laid out in a display case, labelled with their name and year of production. The camera zooms in on one pair of shoes. At this point the mirrored shoes lift off and start to rotate, coasting in space, revealing the various features of the athletic side of the Nike family. We now transition to abstract key elements from various pairs of these classics. Cut back to a butterfly display of the golf shoes. In a similar way we will transition through a series of abstract sequences highlighting the key features of the golf-shoe range. We now introduce an athletic sneaker into the frame, which rotates and combines with the golf shoe, melding together to reveal this new hybrid golf shoe, the SP-5. In addition, if needed, we can tie it further into the print campaign by introducing lines between sneaker/shoe styles.

> **Launch date:** June 2004 > **Media buy info:** Internal presentation and website usage > **Client Company:** Nike > **Creative Director:** Ron Dumas > **Trollbäck & Company:** Director(s) – Joe Wright / Creative director(s) – Joe Wright & Jakob Trollbäck / Designer(s) – Jens Mebes, Todd Neale, Justin Meredith / Producer – Elizabeth Kiehner / Executive Producer – Julie Shevach / Vendor Companies (e.g. music/sound and edit houses) – Singing Serpent, music house / Vendor City, State – San Diego, CA / Camera – Canon EOS 10D / Software – Photoshop, Illustrator, AfterEffects, Final Cut Pro

Shox TL
(Defyun gravitas)

Shox BB4
(Silkorus hoppus)

Air Max
(Airus maximus)

Shox BB4
(Silkorus hoppus)

Shox NZ
(Akurbus impactus)

1975 LDV
(Stylus superioris)

Dri-Fit Tour
(Walkus fairwaya)

Coarse A
(Doglegus)

A Hybrid

Athletics fused with classic golf

A Hybrid

Athletics fused with classic golf

The new evolution in golf footwear

The new evolution in golf footwear.

HOUSE 2 : FANTASY
SECONDHAND LIONS

> DIGITALKITCHEN

SEE ALSO :
> KINGDOM HOSPITAL 026   > NIP/TUCK 044
> THE 6TH DAY 144

> **Executive Creative Director:** Paul Matthaeus > **Creative Directors:** Paul Schneider, Jeff Long > **Designers:** Sevrin Henderson, Ken Kornacki, Mike Jacob, Jason Tang > **3D Designer:** Matt Daly > **Executive Producer:** Don McNeill > **Producer:** Mark Bashore > **Editorial:** Eric Anderson > **Client:** New Line Cinema

HOUSE 2 : FANTASY
SOMETIMES

> PLEIX

SEE ALSO :
> ITSU 092

This is, above all, a work about the dynamics of destructive energy. The origin of the project is, of course, the horrible event of September 11, 2001, but it's also the explosion scene of Zabriskie Point, a Michelangelo Antonioni film. Sometimes is an association of those two visions. We didn't want to make a political point ... Pleix's analysis is simply "physical": from all destructions emerges an evolution.

> **Directed by:** PLEIX > **Music by:** Kid606 (Mille Plateaux) > **Produced by:** PLEIX

This one-minute promotional film is made entirely from existing clips and still imagery from the Getty Images archive. An unusual cast of characters and contexts have been layered and composited together in order to explore the idea of the impossible – the devastation caused by a flying pig. We took inspiration from the turn of phrase "the big idea" – which we thought had plenty of mileage in itself, in relation to who we are and what we do. What we strive to achieve is sort of the impossible, and the idea of attempting to do the impossible led us to another turn of phrase about flying pigs.

> **Directed by:** Julian Gibbs > **Animation/Compositing:** Chris Sayer, Stuart Fortune, Phil Brough, Pete Mellor
> **Offline edit:** Julian Gibbs @ Intro > **Online edit:** Julian Gibbs @ Intro > **Audio:** Julian Gibbs @ IntroMusic:
Extreme Music , Cyclic Trick‰

> INTRO

Intro is a creative company specialising in design and film. Starting in 1988, it has developed a diverse list of clients that span arts and government organisations, advertising agencies and the broadcast sector, as well as the music industry. It reckons its strength resides in "a flexible approach and non-formulaic solutions, so our clients benefit from bespoke design that sets them apart and gets results. We work collaboratively, openly and honestly." Among these clients are the NHS, Elton John, the British Council, The Prodigy, Airbus, Camden Arts Centre, Sony and McCann Erickson. Further examples of Intro's work can be found at www.introwebsite.com.

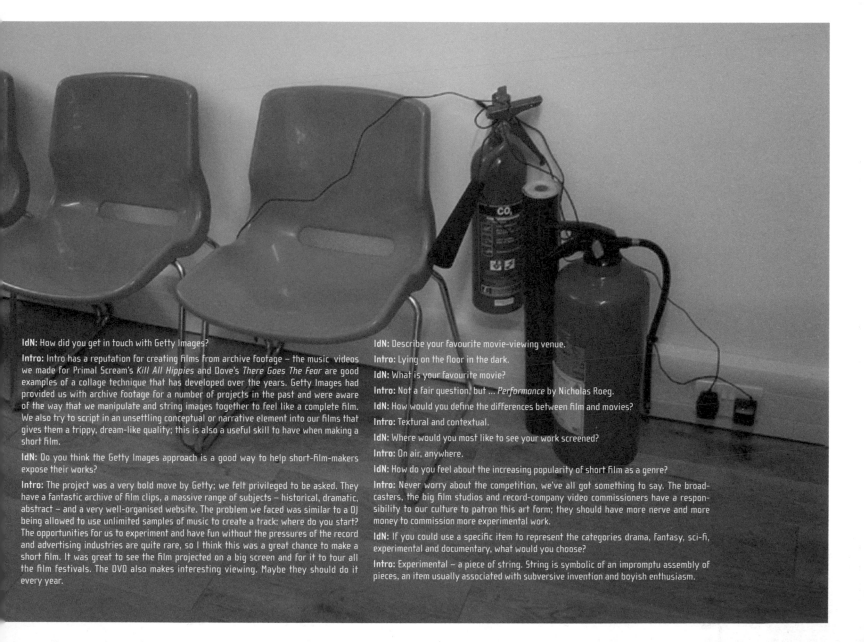

IdN: How did you get in touch with Getty Images?

Intro: Intro has a reputation for creating films from archive footage – the music videos we made for Primal Scream's *Kill All Hippies* and Dove's *There Goes The Fear* are good examples of a collage technique that has developed over the years. Getty Images had provided us with archive footage for a number of projects in the past and were aware of the way that we manipulate and string images together to feel like a complete film. We also try to script in an unsettling conceptual or narrative element into our films that gives them a trippy, dream-like quality; this is also a useful skill to have when making a short film.

IdN: Do you think the Getty Images approach is a good way to help short-film-makers expose their works?

Intro: The project was a very bold move by Getty; we felt privileged to be asked. They have a fantastic archive of film clips, a massive range of subjects – historical, dramatic, abstract – and a very well-organised website. The problem we faced was similar to a DJ being allowed to use unlimited samples of music to create a track: where do you start? The opportunities for us to experiment and have fun without the pressures of the record and advertising industries are quite rare, so I think this was a great chance to make a short film. It was great to see the film projected on a big screen and for it to tour all the film festivals. The DVD also makes interesting viewing. Maybe they should do it every year.

IdN: Describe your favourite movie-viewing venue.

Intro: Lying on the floor in the dark.

IdN: What is your favourite movie?

Intro: Not a fair question, but ... *Performance* by Nicholas Roeg.

IdN: How would you define the differences between film and movies?

Intro: Textural and contextual.

IdN: Where would you most like to see your work screened?

Intro: On air, anywhere.

IdN: How do you feel about the increasing popularity of short film as a genre?

Intro: Never worry about the competition, we've all got something to say. The broadcasters, the big film studios and record-company video commissioners have a responsibility to our culture to patron this art form; they should have more nerve and more money to commission more experimental work.

IdN: If you could use a specific item to represent the categories drama, fantasy, sci-fi, experimental and documentary, what would you choose?

Intro: Experimental – a piece of string. String is symbolic of an impromptu assembly of pieces, an item usually associated with subversive invention and boyish enthusiasm.

The Bonedancer is the title of a film that tells of a birth and even though the name Gints Apsits features in the credits, it is immediately obvious that in reality "there is no story". Because the birth is not only the object but the whole reason for this story's existence. A story that does not tell anything: simply it is, it exists, it manifests itself – and this pervades all of Apsits' works, whether on video or an editorial page. It seems that we participate in the parthenogenic process of creativity in which different styles, techniques and inspirations copulate – or "f**k each other", I would rather say, giving life to a hybrid and heteronomous monster. The dark atmosphere of certain American science-fiction B-movies, the details of the work of Bruegel, the illustrations from erotic postcards or manuals of anatomy from the '50s, the photographs of Witkins or Serrano, the patterns on wallpaper, Buñuel, the creatures of H.R. Geiger, The Rocky Horror Picture Show, Goya ... all are present in the art of Gints Apsits, who, not by chance, is not only the author and director of this film, but also a graphic designer and illustrator – and contributes by giving soul and body, in a non-metaphoric sense, to his obsessions, phobias, deviations and his ancestoral memories. The result is a dense composition, amniotic, ironic and desecrating, in which at least the embryo of an artist navigates, suspended.

> **Director:** Gints Apsits (Latvia) > **Collage artworks:** Gints Apsits > **Animation, edit, fx, graphic design:** Gints Apsits > **Soundtrack:** *TAP* from *WIDE EYED* / Ramon Schneider (Switzerland) and Adam Lieber (South Africa) > **Actors:** Edvin Grasshopperhead, The Mother W340M, Dr. Leonid from st., Fetology hospital, Child The Bonedancer and a lot of reptiles / Produced at FABRICA (Benettons communication and research center - Italy) > **Runing time:** 5.31 min > **Year:** 2002 July

HOUSE 2 : FANTASY

THE BONEDANCER

> GINTS APSITS

SEE ALSO :
> KKF 096

COLLAGE ARTWORKS:
GINTS APSITS

STORY:
THERE ISN'T A STORY.

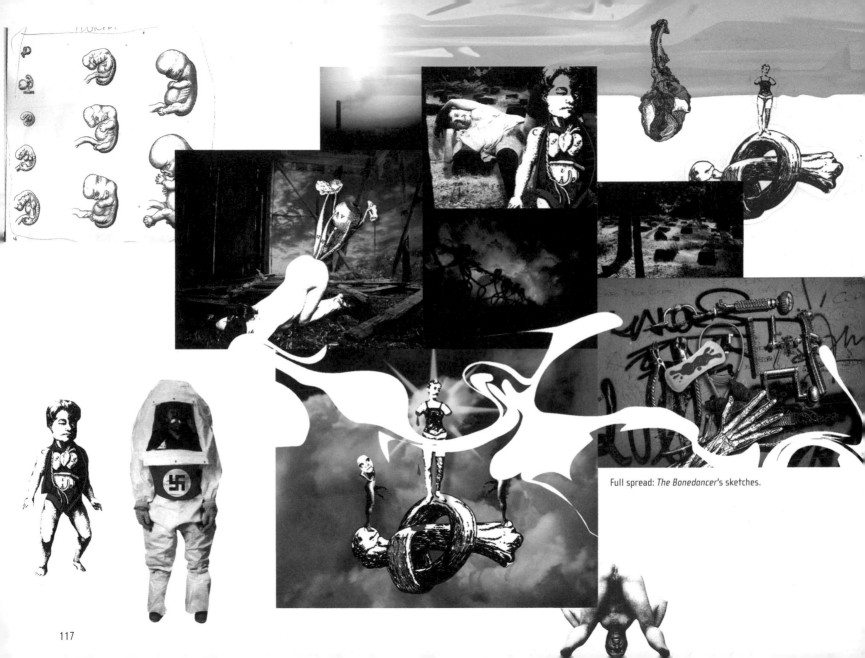

Full spread: *The Bonedancer*'s sketches.

117

This film purposely set out to be the collective vision of the whole Plus et Plus team rather than that of a single person. It's a film that is as thought-provoking as it is strange. In one interpretation, it's a metaphor for the natural cycle of life. However, the film can also be interpreted as a journey of imagination, an idea that continuously grows and morphs into something completely unexpected.

> **Client:** Getty Images (Seattle, WA) > **Co-Founder and Chairman:** Mark Getty > **Co-Founder and CEO:** Jonathan Klein > **Senior Vice President, Creative Customers:** Lewis Blackwell > **Creative Direction:** Chris Ashworth & Tobin Lush > **Project Management:** Nathan Gainford > **Design/Production:** Plus et Plus (New York, NY) > **Director/Designer:** Jeremy Hollister > **Director/Designer:** Judy Wellfare > **Designer/Animator:** Jonathon Leong > **Animator:** Doug Purver > **Animator/Rotoscope:** Artist Ryan McKenna > **Animator/Illustrator:** Jesse Lockwood > **Artist:** Brian Spector Rotoscope > **Producer:** Joy Copeland > **Executive Producer:** Barry Hollister > **Original Music/Sound Design:** Pull (New York, NY) > **Composer:** Mitch Davis > **Executive Producer:** Scott Brittingham > **Hardware/Software:** Discreet *flame, Adobe After Effects, Photoshop and Illustrator, Apple Final Cut Pro

> PLUS ET PLUS

Founded in 2002, Plus et Plus is an innovative creative-services firm whose mission is to energise and motivate audiences through visual design. Broadcasters such as MTV Networks, USA Networks and Voom, the world's first HDTV satellite service, have tapped the studio's expertise in design and direction, editing, visual effects, animation, product design and production. The studio has also worked on spots for Sony Ericsson, Nike, Technics and MAC Cosmetics. The creative team's work has garnered numerous awards including Promax, BDA, i-D., Art Directors Club and International Telly. Plus et Plus is located in New York City at 133 Fifth Avenue.

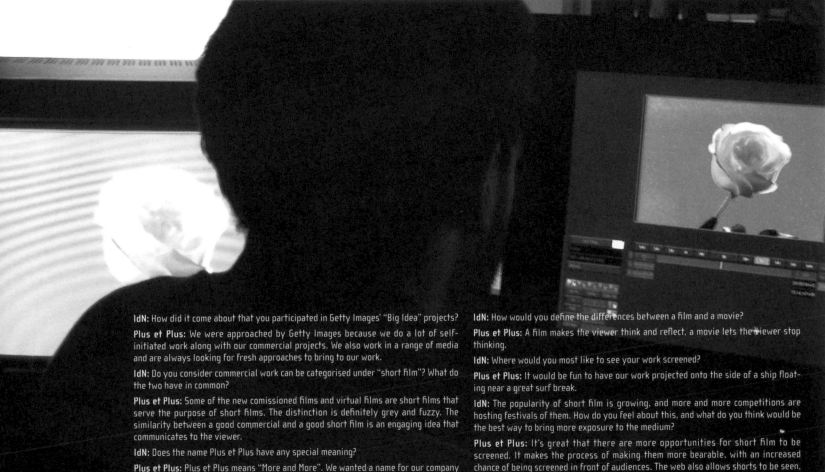

IdN: How did it come about that you participated in Getty Images' "Big Idea" projects?

Plus et Plus: We were approached by Getty Images because we do a lot of self-initiated work along with our commercial projects. We also work in a range of media and are always looking for fresh approaches to bring to our work.

IdN: Do you consider commercial work can be categorised under "short film"? What do the two have in common?

Plus et Plus: Some of the new comissioned films and virtual films are short films that serve the purpose of short films. The distinction is definitely grey and fuzzy. The similarity between a good commercial and a good short film is an engaging idea that communicates to the viewer.

IdN: Does the name Plus et Plus have any special meaning?

Plus et Plus: Plus et Plus means "More and More". We wanted a name for our company that didn't have any visual or stylistic connotations, but a positive meaning. Plus et Plus is an ever-evolving name as we are an ever-evolving company.

IdN: Describe your favourite movie-viewing venue.

Plus et Plus: At home on a lazy, rainy Sunday afternoon.

IdN: What is your favourite movie?

Plus et Plus: We don't have a favourite movie, but movies that inspire us are *Ripley's Game*, *Dangerous Liaisons*, *Last Year At Marionbad*, etc.

IdN: How would you define the differences between a film and a movie?

Plus et Plus: A film makes the viewer think and reflect, a movie lets the viewer stop thinking.

IdN: Where would you most like to see your work screened?

Plus et Plus: It would be fun to have our work projected onto the side of a ship floating near a great surf break.

IdN: The popularity of short film is growing, and more and more competitions are hosting festivals of them. How do you feel about this, and what do you think would be the best way to bring more exposure to the medium?

Plus et Plus: It's great that there are more opportunities for short film to be screened. It makes the process of making them more bearable, with an increased chance of being screened in front of audiences. The web also allows shorts to be seen, but it is more fulfilling to have them seen on big screens.

IdN: If you could use specific items to represent drama, fantasy, sci-fi, experimental and documentary, what would they be?

Plus et Plus: Drama – life; fantasy – dreams; sci-fi – The United States these days; experimental – music; documentary – nature.

HOUSE 3 : SCI-FI

Sci-fi stands for science fiction and is among the most versatile genres of writing. It can encompass a romance, a comedy, a war story, a drama, a mystery – even a Western. The recent *Matrix* series has already become a landmark in sci-fi movie-making, containing outstanding use of technology, high production values and a universal good v. evil struggle.

There are five simple ways to define a sci-fi movie: 1. Any story set in the future, using futuristic technologies as yet unknown; 2. Alternate-world stories, or stories set in a past that contradicts historical fact; 3. Stories set in other worlds; 4. Stories set on Earth before recorded history; 5. Stories that contradict a known or supposed law of nature.

Stories set in worlds that follow our rules are sci-fi. Those set in a universe that doesn't follow our rules are fantasy. A lot of movies fall into both categories. *Star Wars*, for example, takes place in an alternate world – and it also has elements that contradict laws of nature.

HOUSE 3 : SCI-FI
CATWOMAN

> YU+CO.

SEE ALSO :

Patience Philips is a woman who can't seem to stop apologising for her own existence. She works as a graphic designer for Hedare Beauty, a mammoth cosmetics company on the verge of releasing a revolutionary anti-ageing product. When Patience inadvertently happens upon a dark secret her employer is hiding, she finds herself in the middle of a corporate conspiracy. What happens next changes Patience forever. In a mystical twist of fate, she is transformed into a woman with the strength, speed, agility and ultra-keen senses of a cat. With her newfound prowess and feline intuition, Patience becomes Catwoman, a sleek and stealthy creature balancing on the thin line between good and bad. Like any wildcat, she's dangerous, elusive and untamed. Her adventures are complicated by a burgeoning relationship with Tom Lone, a cop who has fallen for Patience but cannot shake his fascination with the mysterious Catwoman, who appears to be responsible for a string of crime sprees plaguing the city.

> **Creative director:** Garson Yu > **Executive producer:** Jennifer Fong > **Producer:** Buzz Hays > **Art director:** Yolanda Santosa > **Animator:** Etsuko Uji > **3D artists:** Chris Vincola and Kamal Hatami > **Shake compositors:** Elika Burns, Robert Cribbett and Jon Doyle > **Conceptual designer:** Edwin Baker > **Editor:** Zachary Scheuren > **Inferno artist:** Danny Mudgett > **Client:** Jean-Christophe 'Pitof' Comar > **Director:** Warner Bros., studio.

HOUSE 3 : SCI-FI

DIE ANOTHER DAY

> FRAMESTORE CFC

The story begins in the demilitarised zone between North and South Korea with a spectacular high-speed hovercraft chase and continues via Hong Kong to Cuba and London where Bond meets up with the two ladies who are to play such important and differing roles in his quest to unmask a traitor and to prevent a war of catastrophic consequence. Hot on the trail of the principle villains, Bond travels to Iceland where he experiences at first hand the power of an amazing new weapon before a dramatic confrontation with his main adversary back in Korea where it all started...

> **Production Company:** Spectre > **Director:** Daniel Kleinman > **Producer:** Johnnie Frankel > **Post Production:** Framestore CFC > **SFX Supervisor:** William Bartlett > **Lead CGI Artists:** Andrew Daffy, Jake Mengers > **CGI Artists:** Simon Stoney, Don Mahmood, Robert Kruppa, Andrew Chapman > **Inferno Artists:** William Bartlett, Avtar Bains, Murray Butler, Ben Cronin > **Matte Artists:** Stephanie Mills, Sophia Tufail > **Editorial:** Roz Lowrie > **R&D:** Alex Parkinson, Tim Aidley > **Technical Support:** Chris Kerr, Dave Carradice, Chi-Kwong Lo, James Studdart > **Post Producers:** Helen MacKenzie, Rebecca Barbour

> FRAMESTORE CFC

Framestore CFC was formed in December 2001 through the union of two of the most creative and dynamic companies in the industry: FrameStore and The Computer Film Company (CFC). The company is now the largest visual effects and computer animation company in Europe, with over 30 years of combined experience in digital film and video technology.

IdN: People tend to over look trailer/ opening titles not knowing a professional company does trailer and opening titles. How would you feel about that?

FCFC: In a way it is a little frustrating. I don't really know why we end up without a credit on the film; it is not like the credits are especially limited. Having said that if we did have a credit it would no doubt be near the end and to be honest the only people who are interested enough to wait that long are likely to find out anyway.

Credits for visual effects artists suffer from this problem in all films. There is a fairly strict universal order of credits which has a long tradition. There were no visual effects in early movies and when they did begin they had very little importance and hence credits were at the end. Nowadays of course the contribution made by the visual effects industry is enormous but the tradition endures.

IdN: Your company is famous for digital film and video technology, do you find any difficulties adding any special visual effect in opening titles?

FCFC: There were of course many challenges to be solved but I think the specific challenge with the Bond title sequence is that it combines technical challenges with aesthetic ones. It is not simply a case of creating something that does not exist and making it look real. It must also look "cool". For example we spent a long time trying different ideas for the "hair" of the molten sun girls. It was not enough for it to look appropriate with the rest of the molten look of the girl, it also had to look "sexy". It is not that easy to make an explosion into something which is recognizable both as long flowing hair and fire at the same time. The two things work against each other. There were many of these sort of problems in the sequence.

IdN: What would be the fun part making an opening title?

FCFC: For me the most interesting part was helping to design the look of the different parts of the sequence. I would speak at length with Daniel Klienman, the director of the titles, about his vision for them. Then I would go away and experiment with various methods and ideas, incorporating both 3D and 2D, as to how to practically generate the images. It was probably the most creative job I have ever done. Also the shoot was quite interesting...

IdN: Describe your most favourite movie-viewing place.

FCFC: Front row of the local cinema with my wife on a Sunday night.

IdN: What is your favourite movie?

FCFC: I wouldn't say I had a favourite movie. If I did I would watch it and watch it again and then I probably wouldn't want to watch it a third time and then I guess it would not be my favourite movie anymore?

One movie I would single out as really inspiring me though was *Who framed Roger Rabbit*. Although it was some time before I got involved in visual effects I always thought of it as being a really amazing film. I had always loved cartoons. Making drawings come to life always seemed like magic to me.

IdN: How would you define the differences between film and movie?

FCFC: I am not sure I understand the question.

Do you mean 'movies' as in blockbusters for the masses, with big budgets, a lot of visual effects, weak stories and implausible dialogue. As opposed to 'films' with low budgets little or no visual effects, moving stories and engaging dialogue?

I think the main difference is to do with effort and accessibility. I think it is true of most art forms that there is a tendency for less accessible work to be ultimately more rewarding. However I like both types of cinema experience. Sometimes you just don't feel in the mood for a 'film'.

IdN: How and where would be your favourite place for your works' screening?

FCFC: To some extent you want your work to be seen by a lot of people so maybe an advert break during the next moon landing would be good. Probably more than that though I think you want to impress your peer group. It is always nice to get work screened at events like Siggraph or at awards ceremonies. I think this is simply because getting good work seen at these events will lead to getting more good work to do.

IdN: If you could use a specific item to represent following categories, drama, fantasy, sci-fi, experimental and documentary. What would be your choice and why?

FCFC: Drama – the moon; Fantasy – the moon; Sc-fi – the moon; Experimental – the moon; Documentary – the moon.

FREE TIBET

> HISAKO HIRAI / FABRICA

SEE ALSO :
> MSA 210

This movie was made for Free Tibet Project event.

> **Illustration and Motion Graphic Design by:** Hisako Hirai
> **Music by:** Suzanne Savage

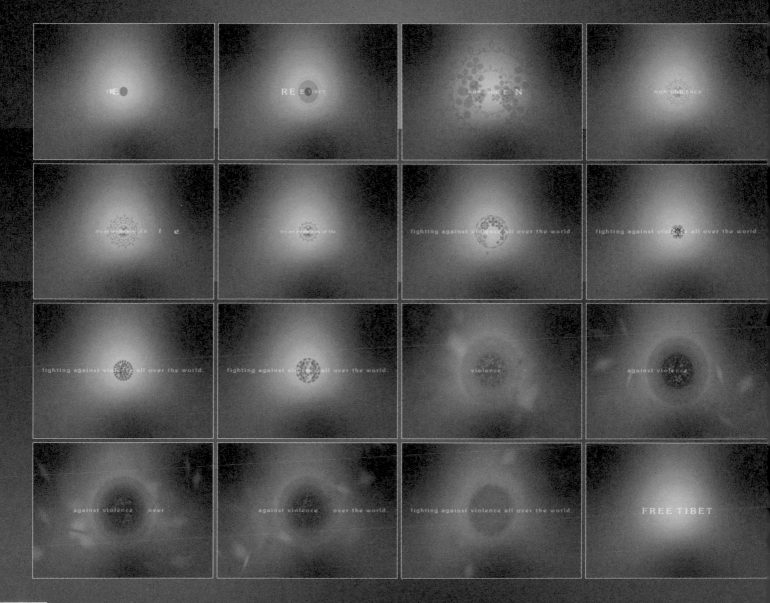

> HISAKO HIRAI / FABRICA

Hisako Hirai was born in Tokyo in 1980. Currently, she is working as a motion-graphic designer, an illustrator and a moviemaker. She will launch her own studio in London in 2005.

IdN: Fabrica is such a well-known creative organisation, even Hollywood would probably love to make a movie with you. If such an approach were made, who would you most like to collaborate with?

HH: I would be interested to work with Francois Ozon. I remember when I saw his film called *See The Sea* for the first time. Seriously, I felt I had been touched by genius. He is so talented. I'd like to make title graphics for his films.

IdN: Describe your favourite movie-viewing venue.

HH: Wherever nobody will disturb me while I'm watching movies.

IdN: What is your favourite movie?

HH: *Der Himmel Über Berlin*.

IdN: How would you define the differences between film and movie?

HH: If I say "film", it means cinema that has a good story. I think "movie" is a more widely used word.

IdN: Where would you most like to see your work screened?

HH: On the wall. By projector.

IdN: How do you feel about the growing popularity of the short-film genre?

HH: I think that increased popularity leads to rising standards.

IdN: If you could use specific items to represent the categories drama, fantasy, sci-fi, experimental and documentary, what would you choose?

HH: Nowadays, fantasy is the most familiar way for me. But I think it depends on the theme.

Imaginary Forces and director Guillermo del Toro join forces once again to creat a main title sequence that unveils the legendary story of Hellboy through a series of tabloid headlines and mysterious photos. In both the film and the comic, the *Hellboy* character has a looming presence in the popular imagination. Like Bigfoot, he is documented through sightings, blurry photos, and questionable news reprtage. Imaginary Forces created their title sequence to establish *Hellboy*'s history as an urban myth. Beginning with a photo taken from the scene of a World War II battle, the camera travels through a gothic "time tunnel". Tabloids and other media fly through the maze-like space each becoming more modern as it gives another angle on *Hellboy*'s existence.

> **Title:** *Hellboy* > **Length:** 1:10 > **Date aired:** April 2 > **Description:** Prolouge, Main and End Title Sequences > **Designed & Produced by:** Imaginary Forces (IF) / Creatice Diector: Peter Frankfurt / Art Director(s): Karin Fong / Designer(s): Grant Lau, Chun-Chien Lien, Karin Fong / Head of Production: Anita Olan / Producer: Keith Bryant / Editor: Justine Gerenstine / Inferno Artist: Andy Dill / 2D Animator(s): Dan Meehan, Andre Fiorini / 3D Animator(s): Chris Pickenpaugh, John Nguyen / Corrdinator(s): Troy Miller > **Studio:** Production Company: Revoution Studios / Director: Guilermo del Toro / Exec. Producer(s): Patrick Plamer / Co-Exec. Producer: Mike Mignola / Producer(s): Lawernce Gordon, Mike Richardson, Lloyd Levin / Post Production Supervisor: Jim Conrads / Editor: Peter Amundson > **Music Company:** Composer: Marco Beltrami

HOUSE 3 : SCI-FI
HELLBOY

> IMAGINARY FORCES

SEE ALSO :

HOUSE 3 : SCI-FI
I, ROBOT

> PICTURE MILL

SEE ALSO :
> THE GRUDGE 058

A mysterious and engaging introduction to Alex Proyas' world of robots gone wrong in *I,Robot*.

Picture Mill leads the audience through a cavernous liquid world that focuses attention forward and down into the depths. A glowing red light is the beacon in the darkness that reveals the title, a reference to a programming change in the robots. The title breaks apart into CG bubbles that integrate into the underwater flashback.

> **Creative Director:** William Lebeda > **Art Director:** David Clayton > **Producer:** Hilary Klarberg > **Designers:** David Clayton, Jose Ortiz, Keith Pang > **3D Animators:** Jon Block, Jose Ortiz > **2D Animators:** Josh Novak, Keith Pang

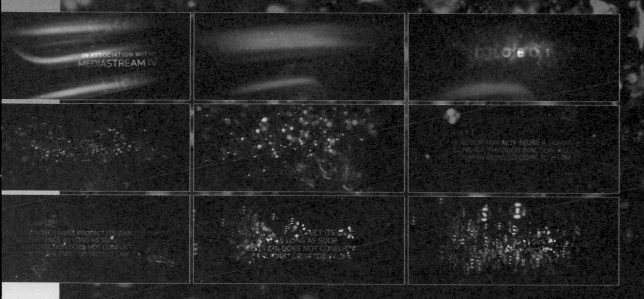

It is a visually astonishing, innovative, narrative short created by David Hayden Schwarz. *ReVision* is proof that compelling stories can be told in the budding genre of Design Cinema – a hybrid form of moving image that is wedged between filmmaking and motion graphics.

It juxtaposes an optometrist who is hypersensitive to the visual world with a blind man who is happily unaware of it. The two meet in a surreal city with a hyper-saturated visual landscape. Through a chance exchange, the optometrist is able see the world anew. His new vision, however, provides more than he bargained for.

As a part of the Design Cinema movement, *ReVision* is the result of the convergence of pre-production, production and post-production. With a single, digital box, artists such as David Schwarz are able to juggle conventional methods of movie-making and invert expectations. Pre-visualisation becomes post-production. Digital-video cinematography melds with graphic design. Animation becomes special effects. The post-artist becomes the content generator.

> **Written, Directed & Designed by:** David Schwarz > **Produced by:** Chloe Ellers > **Director of Photography:** Bobby Eras > **Art Director:** Larissa Desai > **Assistant Director:** Eric Thompson > **Script Supervisor:** Ronny Bagdadi > **Camera Assistant:** Rick Larocca > **Music & Sound Design:** Nate Harrison, Albert Ortega > **Re-recording Mixer:** Kadet Kuhne > **Prop Design:** Shawn Littrell > **Makeup:** Linda Whang > **Additional Writers:** Ronny Bagdadi, Rick Larocca, Jesse Shapira, Richard Statter > **Production Assistants:** Shereen Abdul-Baki, Nikolai Cornell, Ed Johnson, Matt McKissic, Jason Murphy, Syuzi Pakhchyan, Adriana Parcero, Tina Park, Sara Schmidt, Jesse Shapira, Ludmil Trenkov, Kelvin Young

Right and below: *Revision*'s storyboard;
Full spread: *Revision*'s behind the scene

> NOW-SERVING

David H. Schwarz is a designer and director born in New York City in 1977. In 2004, he graduated from the Art Center College of Design in Los Angeles with a masters degree in media design. His thesis focused on "Design Cinema" — the integration of live-action filmmaking and motion graphics.

Before attending the Art Center, he received his Bachelor of Arts from Colgate University. Soon thereafter, he began working as an interactive designer and information architect for a design studio in San Francisco.

Currently, he is involved in a number of projects with his own studio, Now-Serving, that include commercials, music videos, broadcast design, print graphics and media installations. He also writes for a variety of art, design and culture publications. Schwarz is based in Los Angeles, California.

IdN: Why did you name your short film *ReVision*?

DS: The piece has to do with the way we see our world, how as visual makers we are critical of our environment and desire to change it, and how our ideals might not be as perfect as we might imagine. *ReVision* is a play on words and suggests a new way of seeing things, a renewed vision.

IdN: ReVision is a good demonstration of how live action interacts with animation. Did it present any particular difficulties while making it?

DS: Making the piece was a learning experience for everyone involved. I did as much research and testing as I possibly could in order to minimise mistakes during both the live-action shoot and during the post-production process. Naturally, we made tons of mistakes anyway. Lighting the green screen, choice of props, wardrobe, haste during the shoot and the often-heard saying "fix it in post" were all pitfalls. But it's this mix of working in both analog and digital environments – where the unexpected happens – that drives me and suits both sides of my personality well.

IdN: Describe your favourite movie-viewing venue.

DS: Impossible question.

IdN: How would you define the differences between film and movie?

DS: I generally use them interchangeably. However, it's rather clear to me that "film" has a somewhat more archaic feel to it. The word itself evokes a century of film history – which means that it comes with a lot of baggage. "Movie" is much more colloquial and seems to open the genre wide enough to fit this kind of work – that of varying lengths, mixed media and other types of moving images in general. Both, however, seem to suggest the existence of a story line, which is a little disconcerting when we try to fit in visually powerful work such as VJ sets or motion-graphics experiments.

IdN: How and where would you most like to see your work screened?

DS: I would want my film to screen on the desktops of a handful of creative directors/filmmakers whom I admire.

IdN: Short film is becoming increasingly popular and a growing number of festivals and competitions are now hosting this genre. How do you feel about this and what can be done to increase the exposure even more widely?

DS: Festivals such as ResFest and onedotzero are doing a great job of curating experimental short-form moving-image work – from music videos to motion graphics. So those are places helping to gather the crowds and expose an audience to this kind of work. Short-form seems to fit the way we consume media these days and while I regret the loss of our attention span, I also revel in the fact that we can enjoy bits and pieces of media without having to buy into (only) the feature-film experience. I am very happy that many companies seem to be reaching out to curate experimental films to post online (Diesel, Panasonic, etc.) which is another great venue to enjoy short-form content. These venues don't have to abide by prescribed programme durations or interruptions by sponsors, etc. They are unique in that way and I think the sooner that broadcast breaks out of the format, artists making work of varying forms might find a home for it.

IdN: If you had to use specific items to represent the categories drama, fantasy, sci-fi, experimental and documentary, what would you choose?

DS: Drama – a tear; fantasy – a bottomless hole; sci-Fi – a glass tube; experimental – a bubbling beaker; documentary – a facial profile.

THE 6TH DAY

> DIGITALKITCHEN

SEE ALSO :
> KINGDOM HOSPITAL 026   > NIP/TUCK 044
> SECONDHAND LIONS 106

The concept was derived from the film's title (and the fake history developed to support this; represented by the dates and events). A visual representation of the events leading to human cloning was shown through historians' POV (operating a future version of todays microfiche). All title imagery was created digitally or by stills. Cellular footage was created in After Effects, other scenes were filled out with stock photos and many of the foetus stills were shot by DK (placing cow foetuses in an aquarium, and then animating the environment).

> **Executive Creative Director:** Paul Matthaeus > **Designers:** Scott Hudziak, Brian Short, Danny Yount, Mason Nicoll, Jay Bryant > **Producer:** Lane Jensen > **Editorial:** Eric Anderson > **Client:** Columbia Pictures / Phoenix Pictures

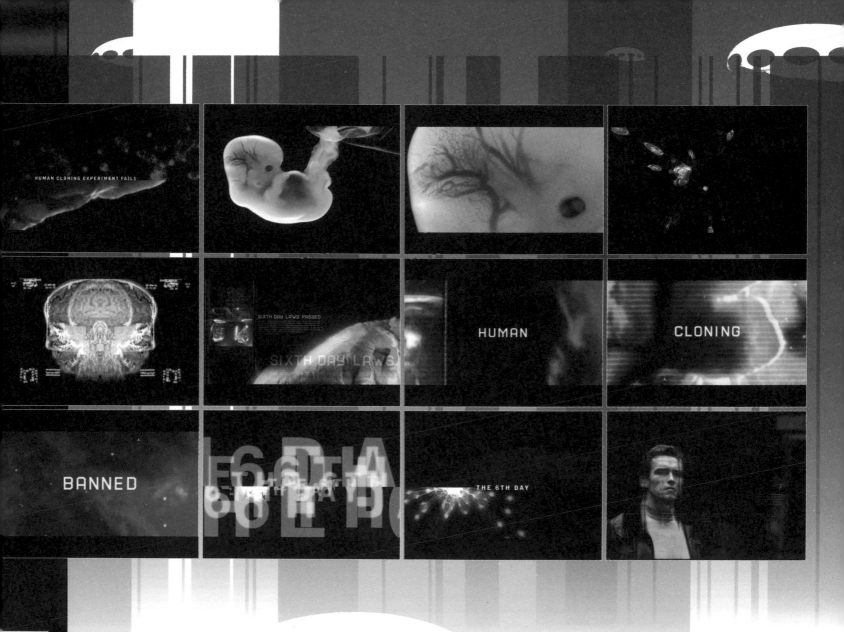

HOUSE 3 : SCI-FI

THE CHRONICLES OF RIDDICK

> 4U+CO.

A UNIVERSAL PICTURES
PRESENTATION

COLM FEORE

It is a dark time in the universe. Planet after planet is falling to an unholy army of Necromongers – conquering warriors who offer ravaged worlds a simple choice: convert or die. Those who refuse their rule hope in vain for someone or something that will slow the spread of Necromongers. But rebels are short-lived and saviours, it seems, are in short supply. When things get bad, weary survivors turn to myths for comfort – murmured prophecies, vain hopes, legends of good vanquishing evil. But good isn't always the antidote to evil and legends can be wrong. Sometimes the only way to stop evil is not with good – but with another kind of evil. So an unlikely figure is summoned from exile and asked to join the fight: Riddick, who couldn't care less who's in charge of the universe, just as long as he's left alone. Since leaving a god-forgotten (and creature-ridden) planet in the Tauras system five years ago, the wanted fugitive hasn't looked back. Most of the time has been spent evading capture and ghosting whatever mercenaries are on his tail. To him, it's all the same, apocalypse or no – this one-man army is interested only in saving his own life. Get in his way and he'll gladly take yours. But something has been set in motion, and the coming confrontation propels Riddick into a series of epic, winner-take-all battles: from an idyllic, multicultural civilisation under siege; to a subterranean prison carved beneath the surface of a hellish, volcanic planet; and finally, aboard the massive baroque Necro mother ship and the seat of power in their black empire – the Basilica. In the final battle, it is foretold that the fate of all may depend upon the destiny of one Furyan.

> **Creative director:** Garson Yu > **Executive producer:** Jennifer Fong > **Producer:** Buzz Hays > **Designer:** Synderela Peng
> **2D animator:** David Yan > **3D artists:** Chris Vincola and Nate Homan > **Editor:** Zachary Scheuren > **Inferno artist:**
Danny Mudgett > **Client:** David Twohy > **Director:** Universal Pictures, studio.

VIN DIESEL

PRODUCED BY
SCOTT KROOPF
VIN DIESEL

THE CHRONICLES OF
RIDDICK

HOUSE 3 : SCI-FI

THE HITCHHIKER'S GUIDE TO THE GALAXY

> IMAGINARY FORCES

SEE ALSO :

Beginning with a dramatic camera pull-back from the Earth, accompanied by Louis Armstrong's "What a Wonderful World", Imaginary Forces created a fully orginal teaaser/trailer to premiere at 2004's Comicon in San Diego. Keeping with the irony and humor of the film, the mood is dramatically altered when the Earth explodes and the giant words "Don't Panic" flash across the screen. Traveling through the debris, we arrive in an open space where the stars converge to form both the logo and hitchhiking thumb from the original books and television series, but with a cleaner, more modern approach.

> **Title:** *Hitchhiker's Guide to the Galaxy* comican teaser > **Length:** 1:15:29 > **Date aired:** Premiering at Comicon on Friday, July 23 at 2:30 PM at the Incredibles panel discussion as a surprise element .. > **Description:** Teaser (we developed the concept, development and execution) > **Designed & Produced by:** Imaginary Forces (IF) / Creative Director: Peter Frankfurt / Art Director(s): Brain Mah / Designer(s): Brian Mah / Head of Production: Anita Olan / Editor: Danielle White / Inferno Artist: Andy Dill / 3D Animator(s): Sean Koriakin, Charles Khoury, Chris Pickenpaugh / Coordinator(s): Troy Miller / Studio: Walt Disney Studio

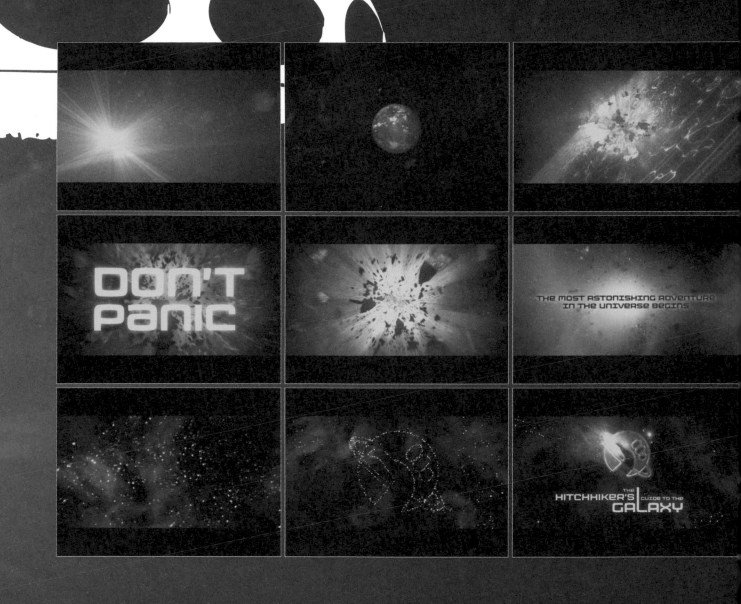

THE LADY LOVELACE

> UVPHACTORY

In the near future, an artificial-intelligence product is released that enables people to interact with the hologram of a beautiful woman. As we follow two neighbours simultaneously manipulating the virtual woman, an unexpected power outage cuts short their interactions and forces them back to their real physical environments.

> **CAST:** *Lady Lovelace* – Rachel Sledd / Frank Milton – John Dacunto / Seymour Adams – Fletcher Allen
> **Director & Writer:** Alexandre Moors > **Producer:** Jonathan Lia > **Executive Producer:** Emmanuelle Moors
> **Director of Photography:** Aaron Phillips > **Production Designer:** Nicholas Feldman > **Editor:** Jonathan Nigro > **Music:** Murat > **First Assistant Director:** Ariel Danziger > **Sound Recordist:** Ralph Miccio > **3d Artists:** Carl Mok, Dave Bernardin > **Special Effects:** Alexandre Moors

THE *Lady Lovelace*

DECEPTION SYSTEM

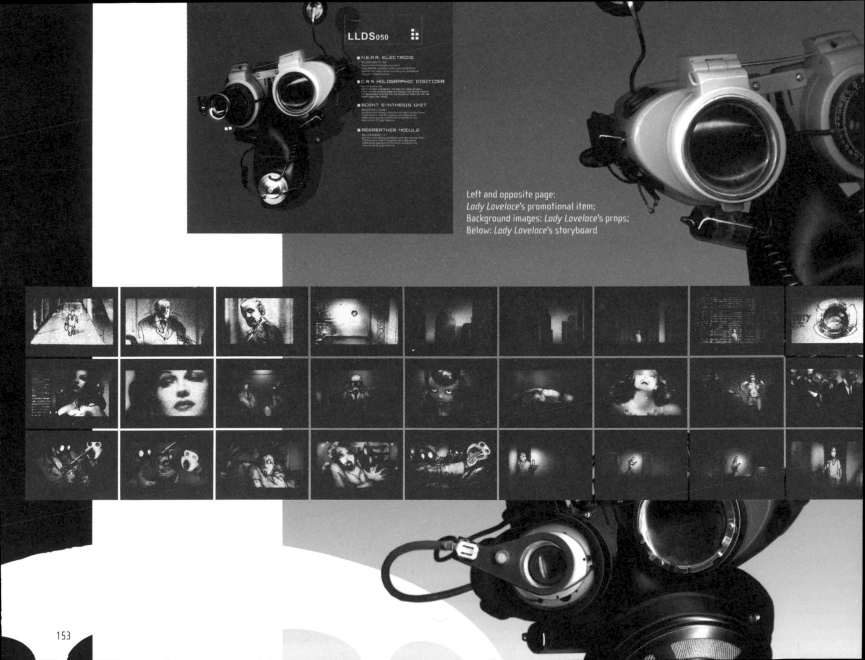

LLDS050

■ H.E.R.R. ELECTRODE

■ C.R.S HOLOGRAPHIC DIGITIZER

■ SCENT SYNTHESIS UNIT

■ REBREATHER MODULE

Left and opposite page:
Lady Lovelace's promotional item;
Background images: *Lady Lovelace*'s props;
Below: *Lady Lovelace*'s storyboard

> UVPHACTORY

Alexandre Moors was born in Paris in 1972 and attended the Ecole Nationale Superieure des Arts Decoratifs (ENSAD), where he began experimenting with interactive story-telling. Moving to New York in 1998, he worked as a broadcast designer and creative director for Streetsound, the electronic-music channel on the Pseudo Online Network. *The Lady Lovelace Deception System* is his second short film. Today, Alexandre is working as creative director of the design company UV/Phactory.

IdN: As well as making short films, you also produce TV main titles: are there any big differences in term of production between these two different media?

AM: I always try to make my short-film titles very sober, almost minimalistic, so they don't overshadow the film. Working for TV would be just the opposite: titles can or should be better, at least in term of visual quality, than whatever comes next.

IdN: Do you think MTV could be considered as short film?

AM: We're actually making a music video right now for the band TV On The Radio that could be seen as a short film. And I'm sure *Lady Lovelace* could work on MTV as well. I guess the difference comes down to dialogue.

IdN: What is the fun part of making an opening title?

AM: Making it into a little short film in itself. I guess *se7en* is still the reference for that.

IdN: Describe your favourite movie-viewing venue.

AM: A New York theatre with balcony seats.

IdN: What is your favourite movie?

AM: *Come And See*, directed by Elem Klimov.

IdN: How would you define the difference between film and movie?

AM: A film is a work of art, a movie is a piece of commercial entertainment.

IdN: Where would you most like to see your work screened?

AM: In movie theatres around the world. I was lucky in that way with *Lady Lovelace*, which screened in Cape Town, Tokyo, New York, London, etc. because of the Resfest short-film festival.

IdN: Short films are becoming more and more popular and there are an increasing number of festivals and competitions hosting them. How do you feel about this and what more do you think can be done to increase people's exposure to short film?

AM: Short films are becoming more popular, but there are fewer and fewer places to watch them lately. The US and French TV networks – the two markets I know best – have almost completely stopped buying them. I believe TV is the best way to discover shorts. The best situation is if programmes start after 1am, which is a time where you're open to watching just about anything.

HOUSE 3 : SCI-FI

THIS IS THE CREATURE INSIDE

> BEN TSENG / FABRICA

SEE ALSO:
> THE CUBE 228

An imaginary journey inside the world of the color test pattern.

> **Director:** Ben Tseng Ho Fung > **Music, artist:** Miss Kittin & The Hacker
> **Written and produced by:** Caroline Herve & Michel Amato > **Record company:**
International Deejay Gigolo Records > **Published by:** Sub/Edition Gigolo

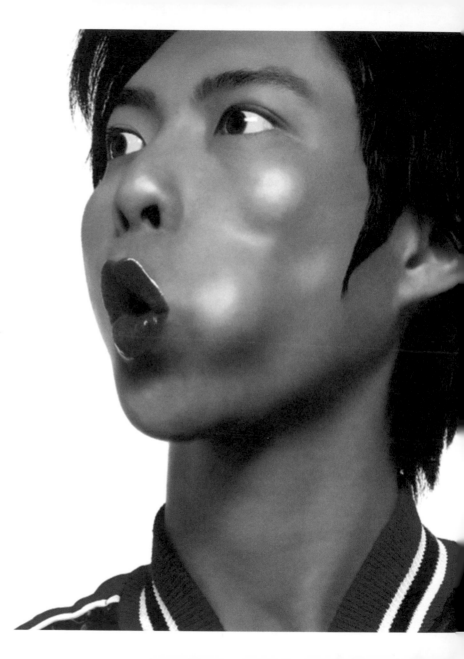

> BEN TSENG / FABRICA

Ben Tseng was born in Hong Kong in 1979. From 1997-99 he studied art and design at Hong Kong Polytechnic University. Afterwards he went to London and took a BA graphics and media design course at the London College of Printing. He specialised in moving images. His work was shown in exhibitions and competitions, including "Unleash The Talent Inside", a short-film competition held by Channel 4 in the UK in 2001; "Xhibit", an annual exhibition held by the London Institute, in 2001; and "Uncut", a short-film exhibition at the ICA in London in 2002. After college he started working as a freelance. He worked for the company The Light Surgeons on various projects, including short films, commercials and live performances. Since January 2004 he has been working at Fabrica.

IdN: Describe your favourite movie-viewing venue.

BT: There is no doubt that watching films in the cinema is great. However, watching movies can also be a private activity that I would like to enjoy alone. Therefore, I think my favourite place to watch a film is in a house with a nice projection screen, good sound system, possibly air conditioning and snacks. And can I have a few friends – but no-one who talks a lot, please.

IdN: What is your favourite movie?

BT: There are a lot, but the two I watch again and again are *Buffalo 66* by Vincent Gallo and *Goddess Of 1967* by Clara Law.

IdN: How would you define the differences between film and movies?

BT: I think "film" and "movie" have the same meaning. Video is different.

IdN: Where would you most like to see your work screened?

BT: On television.

IdN: How do you feel about the growing popularity of the short-film genre, and what more can be done to increase exposure to it?

BT: It's good. Digital technology brings the possibility for people to make their own video and nowadays you can see a lot of amazing stuff on the Internet or at film festivals. Since we do not need big budgets and many people to produce a video, it allows us to express our own ideas without much restriction. Yes, it is very competitive, but I think that is good and it brings positive energy for people to create better and better stuff. Film festivals are very useful for short-film exposure. Also, products such as the *FLIPS'* DVD are good because people can actually buy it and watch it whenever they want. I am trying to collect all these products.

IdN: If you could use specific items to represent the categories drama, fantasy, sci-fi, experimental and documentary, what would you choose?

BT: Drama – sweet-and-sour chicken. It is always sweet and sour, sometimes too much so. Fantasy – gum. It tastes good, but it's not real, you can't keep it forever. Sci-fi – instant food. Reminds me of the future. Experimental – some weird food I've never tried. Documentary – rice and bread. The fundamentals.

HOUSE 3 : SCI-FI
THUNDERBIRDS

> NEXUS PRODUCTIONS LTD

SEE ALSO :
> CATCH ME IF YOU CAN 008   > FIZZY EYE 084
> MIRANDA 034

RON COOK

Nexus directors Smith & Foulkes have created an animated sequence for Working Title's feature film *THUNDERBIRDS* based on the British cult puppet series of the sixties, starring Sir Ben Kingsley, Bill Paxton, and Sophia Myles. Nexus were asked to craft a title sequence that captured the light hearted tone of the movie, but also gave context and background information to a US audience not familiar with International Rescue and their dramatic endeavours.

> **Main Titles by:** Nexus Productions > **Created by:** Smith & Foulkes > **Produced by:** Chris O'Reilly and Charlotte Bavasso > **Head of 2D:** Reece Millidge > **Head of 3D:** Darren Price > **Technical Director:** Rob Andrews > **Production Manager:** Juliette Stern > **2D animation:** Graham Bebbington, Stuart Doig, David Bunting > **3D modelling and animation:** Michael Greenwood, Brad Noble > **Compositors:** Matthew Hood, Lee Lennox > **2D assistant:** Kwok Fung Lam

HOUSE 4 : DOCUMENTARY

Any home video could be categorised as a documentary, the documentary being a non-fiction film depicting real-life situations, usually with individuals describing their feelings and experiences. The documentary film is concerned with truth and reality. The term documentary evokes the notion in the viewer that what appears on screen is factually based. In another words, the role of the documentary is to present facts objectively without editorialising or inserting fictional matter, as in a document or file.

Under the guise of capturing reality/truth, documentaries can manipulate the viewer into identifying with certain ideologies and groups/individuals. Michael Moore's latest film, *Fahrenheit 911*, for example, "documents" a conspiracy on the part of US President George Bush, who is revealed as having had close relationships with terrorists and using the defence of his own country's safety as an excuse to attack other countries. As a documentary, what it shows is real enough. But once it's been edited, and narration, music and sound-effects added, it becomes a point of view. The truth is — there is no complete truth. It's the same as looking at the moon — you'll only ever see a part of it, never the whole thing.

DOCUMENTARY

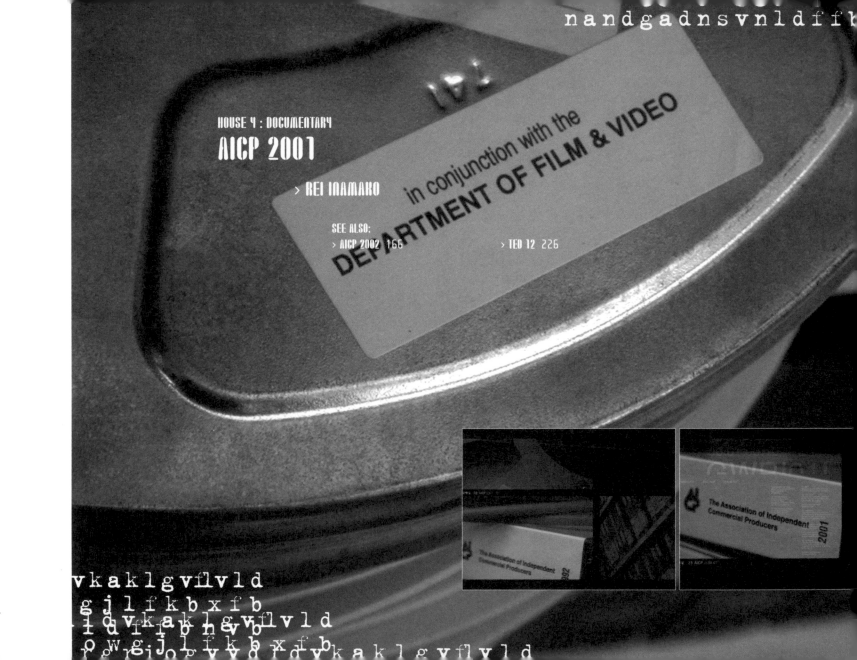

HOUSE 4 : DOCUMENTARY

AICP 2001

> REI INAMAKO

in conjunction with the
DEPARTMENT OF FILM & VIDEO

SEE ALSO:
> AICP 2002 165   > TED 12 226

The Association of Independent
Commercial Producers

2001

The Association of Commercial Producers (AICP) holds an annual awards event at the Metropolitan Museum of Art in New York City to celebrate the art and craft of commercial making. The *AICP 2001* title sequences were shown to an audience of 1,800 commercial producers and directors. To commemorate the 10th anniversary of the AICP, the concept of the piece is based around the idea of "archive", creating a title sequence that metaphorically serves as an imaginary microfiche. The title sequences include the main opening title for the entire show as well as vignettes, which served as the introduction for individual categories.

> **Director:** Rei Inamoto > **Designers:** Jerome Austria, Leslie Karavil, Garry Waller > **Special Effects Artist:** Danny Gonzalez > **Editor:** Brandon Werner > **Music:** Sacred Noise > **Agency:** R/GA

For the title sequence of *AICP 2002*, the concept was "the light in commercial making." Using various devices and techniques that employ light as part of commercial making, the opening title sequence visually captures the essence of the process. Individual vignettes also metaphorically portray each category effectively and poetically.

> **Director:** Rei Inamoto > **Designers:** David Alcorn, Nathan Iverson, Jean Kapp, David Morrow, Yzabelle Munson, Len Small, Garry Waller > **Special Effects Artist:** Danny Gonzalez > **Editor:** Brandon Werner > **Editing Assistant:** Marcia Bernard > **Videographers:** Danny Gonzalez, Nathan Iverson, Stephen Barnwell, Garry Waller > **Music:** Sacred Noise > **Agency:** R/GA

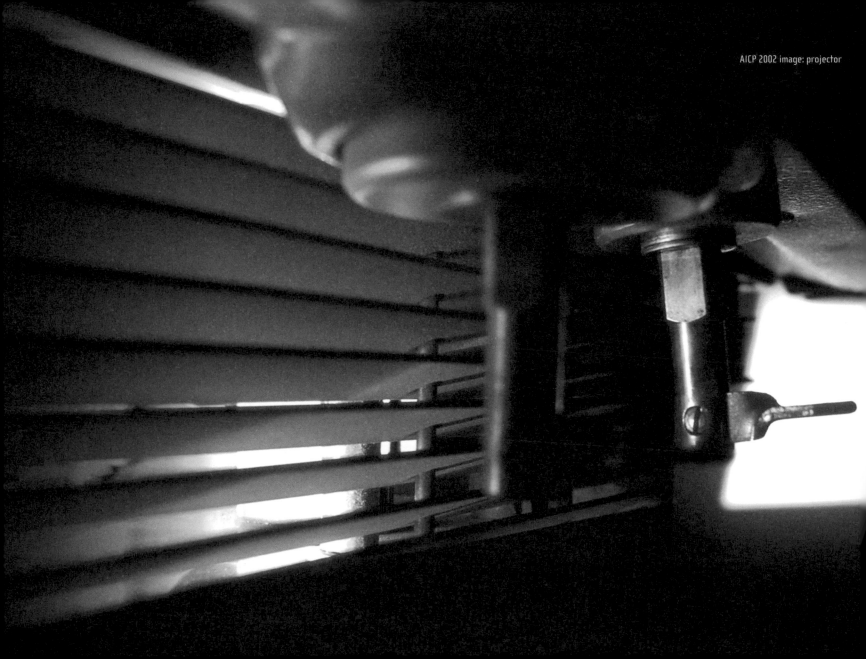

a d s f d f l a w f j r g r i o g v v d l d v k a k l g v
f v d v g g a j r g g i d g a w o w g i l f k h x f h f
r i

THE ASSOCIATION

PRODUCERS

THE ASSOCIATION

THE MUSEUM OF MODERN ART NEW YORK
presents

THE MUSEUM OF MODERN ART NEW YORK

Art & Techniqu

AMERICA

MERI

TELEV

The Art & Technique of
THE AMERICAN TELEVISION COMMERCIAL

> REI INAMAKO

Born in Tokyo, Rei grew up in the deep mountains of central Japan, climbing trees and playing with wild animals. In his childhood, he dreamed of becoming the next Jackie Chan and/or Maradona. At the age of 14, however, Rei discovered the pleasure of the craft of art and design and decided to shift his focus. He still maintains his quiet passion for kung-fu and the beautiful game of soccer.

During his late teens and early 20s, Rei travelled around the globe in search of a perfect place/way to spend the rest of his life. For now, he resides in Brooklyn, New York, serves as creative director at AKQA (http://www.akqa.com), and frequently collaborates with Tronic (www.tronicstudio.com). His favourite beverage is mango smoothie.

IdN: What triggers your great passion for short-film-making?

RI: Film allows you to tell an idea over time. It also allows you to tell it visually and tell it with sound. Unlike traditional graphic design, which relies more heavily on visual itself and not necessarily on sound, film touches multiple senses that human beings have. I'm interested in designing experience and film is one step towards multi-sensory experience.

IdN: The short films you have submitted for *FLIPS 8 – Moview* are all your own projects; what inspired you to make them?

RI: The films that I submitted were created as opening title sequences for events. For each piece, there was a clear idea to express visually. For *AICP 2001*, the idea was "archive", for *AICP 2002*, "the light", and for *TED 12*, "film". Those core ideas became the very starting point for them and throughout the execution, the idea was the guiding principle.

IdN: Describe your favourite movie-viewing venue.

RI: My own apartment.

IdN: What is your favourite movie?

RI: *Delicatessen* by Marc Caro and Jean-Pierre Jeunet.

IdN: How would you define the differences between film and movie?

RI: I see "film" as an artistic endeavour, whereas "movie" is a commercial pursuit. In other words, filmmakers make films to express an idea, a point of view. Moviemakers make movies to make money.

IdN: Where would you most like to see your work screened?

RI: In a public space.

IdN: The short-film genre is growing in popularity, with an increasing number of festivals and competitions devoted to it. How do you feel about this?

RI: I think it's good and bad. It's good because more competition urges film-makers to create better work. It's bad because of the popularity – there are more people doing it, which leads to more mediocre work.

IdN: What would be the most effective way of gaining more exposure for the short-film form?

RI: With the advent of the Internet, short films are already getting a lot more exposure than they used to. Also, there are numerous short-film festivals, such as ResFest, onedotzero, etc., which give a platform for unknown filmmakers to expose their work. So, these two vehicles of communication are the most effective way for more exposure.

IdN: If you could use specific items to represent the categories drama, fantasy, sci-fi, experimental and documentary, what would you choose?

RI: Drama – a bed. Someone once said: "Making love is the most beautiful thing human beings do. We do it in the dark and do it with our eyes closed." That's a drama. Fantasy – a snow globe. A snow globe is a world – a fantastical one – within such a confined space. A great setting for creating a fantasy. Sci-fi – a monitor. A monitor provides a way to create an alternate reality. An alternate reality is a basis for many sci-fi stories and can be a powerful vehicle to tell a sci-fi story. Experimental – a Lomo camera. It would be interesting to create an experimental film shot entirely on a Lomo camera. Documentary – a non-fiction book. When I read books, I tend to be interested less in novels and fiction than in non-fiction and real stories. A non-fiction book provides a great starting point for a documentary.

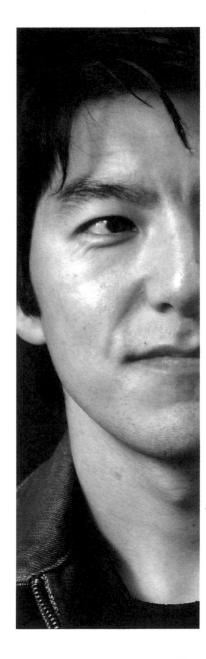

HOUSE 4 : DOCUMENTARY

BEAUTIFUL LOSERS

> SARTORIA COMUNICAZIONE

ogvvdldvkakIgvllvld

xbxfb
bnvb
grogwrt

ad
fv
na

adsfdl
fvdvg
nand

nan

Beautiful Losers is a trailer for a full-length documentary based
on a new wave of American artists working outside the traditional
art community. As much as it is about art, Beautiful Losers is
about cultural politics, freedom of expression, and difference.

> Project by: Sartoria.com > Creative direction: Giorgio de Mitri > Camera:
Claudia Tosi, Marco Molinelli > Words: Mode2, Lara Gilmore > Editor: PaoloFreschi
> Transcripts: Manuel Maggio > Special thanks to the curators, all the artists and
Todd Jordan for images taken from the skate.

ld
fb

vnia dffbnvb
173
g g ggsklgrogwrt

Sartoria is a tight-knit group of artists, designers and cultural architects whose credo is: "Sartoria does not make traditional suits. After all, one size does not fit all. Sartoria tailors custom-fit images with speed and accuracy. From designing multimedia communication tools to redefining brand strategy; from producing installations, events and publications to practising guerilla marketing."

IdN: Why did you call your work *Beautiful Losers*? Is there any hidden meaning in it?

SC: The meaning is not hidden at all. *Beautiful Losers* is the title of an exhibition and a book curated by Aaron Rose and Christian Strike. The exhibition opened at the Contemporary Arts Center, Cincinnati in March 2004. It travelled to the Yerba Buena Center for the Arts, San Francisco during the summer of 2004 and is destined for other US cities in the future.

The "Beautiful Losers" exhibition surveys the production of a group of artists working outside mainstream culture. The catalogue describes this group of artists as "... state-of-the-art-bohemian poets, underground music heroes, revolutionary skaters, graffiti kings and queens, as well as artists." That description fits the atmosphere of the exhibition as well.

What distinguishes this artistic movement from others is not the content nor the form but the context of the work. It has a direct relation to underground culture: music, graffiti, graphics, skateboarding, and so on. These artists have chosen to work outside the rational white walls of the art world. They purposefully explore new spaces to exhibit their work (community projects, billboards, buildings, zines, record covers, T-shirts, posters, skateboards, etc.) aiming to reach out to a diversified public rather than catering to the exclusive boundaries of the art world.

IdN: What was the initial idea behind making *Beautiful Losers*?

SC: The reason behind making *Beautiful Losers* was to provide a showcase for this special group of artists and enrich the experience of the outstanding work and the incredible people behind the project. Sartoria has been interested in this group of artists for the past 10 years. *Beautiful Losers* is a cohesive and important body of work that reflects a significant cultural shift in the direction of American art.

IdN: Do you think there are certain filming methods that have to be used in order to categorise a short film as a documentary?

SC: This project is a trailer for a more in-depth documentary.

IdN: Describe your favourite movie-viewing venue.

SC: There is no better place to watch a film than at the theatre.

IdN: What is your favourite movie?

SC: There are too many to mention.

IdN: Where would you most like to see your work screened?

SC: I would like to see *Beautiful Losers* as a trailer on the web, a full-length documentary on DVD or screened in a gallery or in a theatre.

IdN: The popularity of short film is growing, with an increasing number of festivals and competitions hosting the genre. How do you feel about this and what do you think needs to be done to increase the exposure even further?

SC: The quality, content and energy are what make a film work, not the length. I am an editor more than a filmmaker. I try to give the same feeling and attention to everything I do.

HOUSE 4 : DOCUMENTARY
FLY IN

> FLYING MACHINE

SEE ALSO:
> SILENCE 186

Fly In is a video short that explores the tranquillity of routine. By focusing on the ritualistic movements of workers in India, the film celebrates the beauty of detail, and the richness and meaning that can be found in even the simplest of tasks.

> **Directed by:** flyingmachine > **Photography:** Sharone Ben Harosh
> **Editor:** Ariel Roubinov > **Composer:** Keren Rosenbaum

177

> FLYING MACHINE

Flying Machine is a New York-based creative design and art hub. Working within a variety of media, the studio creates visual solutions for entertainment, advertising and branding. Founder and creative director Micha Riss has produced award-winning results for a broad range of international clientele.

IdN: Why are you so interested in making short films?

FM: We are as interested in making films as we are in designing posters or T-shirts. To us, there really is no difference. Filmmaking is design. At Flying Machine, our mantra is that creative thinking is everything. It all begins with an idea that, when executed, dictates its own style. We are most interested in communicating.

IdN: Describe your favourite movie-viewing venue.

FM: We think movies are most magical when viewed outdoors. It would be nice if there were still drive-in movie theatres like there were during the 1950s. There was also a time when features used to be screened with a short film, or a cartoon, playing first. In New York City during the summers, we have a weekly series of classic films where thousands of people gather in a park with their friends and picnic blankets. This is the most wonderful power of filmmaking – it brings people together in a social experience.

IdN: What is your favourite movie?

FM: We don't have favourites, only things we really love. We are inspired by talented people such as Chris Cunningham, Kubrick, Malevich, Rodechenko and Björk, just to name a few at random.

IdN: How would you define the differences between film and movie?

FM: It's purely a question of semantics. A film is a movie. A movie is a painting. A painting is a design. A design is an idea.

IdN: Where would you most like to see your work screened?

FM: Films look best projected very large. We want many people to see the things we make, not just a select few standing around a white room. It would be nice to see our work projected on the sides of large buildings around the world.

IdN: How do you feel about the newfound popularity of short film as a genre?

FM: This is a good thing. More places for viewing films means more people will be able to see different kinds of films, and more people will be inspired to make their own films. Then the world will be a happier place.

IdN: What do you think is the most effective way of increasing the exposure of short films?

FM: There are two big points here. First, some countries make funding for short films a priority, and some don't. Art defines culture, and without enough arts funding, the culture suffers. Second, while the Internet has made it easier to see great work, it is not yet an ideal place to view short films. Too often resolution is sacrificed for exposure. Over time, we hope these technical problems will be resolved. Eventually, the television and the computer could merge, and then things will be really interesting.

HOUSE 4 : DOCUMENTARY
FOOTSTEP

> ADOLESCENT

新宿・橋瀬 方面

EXPRESS   SHINJUKU   20:58   10
LOCAL   SHINJUKU   21:05   6

a d
f v
n a

A young creative lives and works in Tokyo and New York city, *Footstep* is a piece inspired by the people living in chaotic city "Tokyo".

> **Visual:** Mina Muto from adolescent > **Photos:** Mina Muto from adolescent, helloharuo.com, Roger Clark > **Music by:** Pete Namlook & Burhan Öçal > All rights reserved by Mina Muto, 2004

> ADOLESCENT

WM-251CW

¥32800

Headed by Man-Wai Cheung and Mina Muto, adolescent focuses on producing unique, thought-provoking images that will accurately communicate any message to the world.

Based in New York with an international presence, neither trends nor borders dictate our work.

We love to explore and experiment with different themes and ideas; we have never been limited by today's flavour. We strive to make our images inspire thought into action.

The team has put this principle into action through their work with Nickelodeon (USA), SVT1 (Sweden) and Digital Vision (UK).

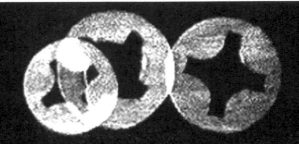

IdN: What triggers you having such great passion toward short filmmaking?

MM (Mina Muto): It just came naturally, I couldn't stop creating it. When you are in the middle of it you don't know what it is, that was a raw passion and energy to create I never felt that strongly before. I was driven.

IdN: The style and story behind the *Footstep* is really unique, why did you choose this filming method/ way of story telling?

MM: It should be unique because it's a very personal piece. I have chosen the photo animation because it was perfect to create the atmosphere of my memories.

IdN: Describe your most favourite movie-viewing place.

MM/MWC (Man Wai): Home!!! with lots of munchies...

IdN: What is your favourite movie?

MM: I must say *The Goonies* (1985) gave me the dream!

MWC: *Moulin Rogue* (2001)

IdN: How would you define the differences between film and movie?

MM: Movie is easier to pronounce.

IdN: How and where would be your favourite place for your works' screening?

MM: ...it would be great to have a screening in Yakushima island in Japan!

IdN: The popularity of short film is getting higher and higher, more and more competitions of short film are being hosted. As a creator of short film, how you feel about that? From your point of view what would be the most effective and useful way to allow more and more short film exposure?

MM/MWC: We are very excited about new generation and technology. People's life style has changed dramatically and it will be easier to view more movies and films online at home!

IdN: If you could use a specific item to represent the following categories, drama, fantasy, sci-fi, experimental and documentary. What would be your choice and why?

MM/MWC: Documentary and experimental. We want to express something more personal.

A shared monologue explores the often invisible and silent unity among strangers, while evoking the solitude of everyday life.

> **Producer:** flyingmachine > **Director:** Keith Ehrlich > **Editor:** Terence Ziegler > **Director of photography:** Daniel McKeown

HOUSE 4 : DOCUMENTARY

SILENCE

> FLYING MACHINE

SEE ALSO:
> FLY IN 176

adsfdflawfjrgriogvvdldvkaki

f b n v b -
fingriogvvdldvkaklgvflvld
adsfdflawfjrgriogvvdldvkaklgvflvld

HOUSE 5 : EXPERIMENTAL

Experimental films are sometimes put down by those who don't like them as being self-indulgent, elitist and boring — and having very little to do with experimentation. But the word "experiment" doesn't only carry technical implications — it can refer to the spirit in which the film is made. Since such movies are mainly the work of individual auteurs, rather than major studios, they usually afford maximum freedom to those making them. Hence the increased possibilities of failure compared with movies made in a more tightly structured context.

One of the earliest films to be dubbed "experimental" was a 10-minute effort by Norman McLaren called *A Chairy Tale* (1957). This told the story of a man attempting to sit on a "reluctant" chair, through the process of live action filming and frame-by-frame pixilation. Experimental cinema carries connotations that it challenges the fixed boundaries between ideas and art forms, presenting infinite possibilities in terms of action, presentation, lighting, etc. Inspiration is everything.

GENERAL INSTRUCTIONS FOR
"10 Degrees to Sundan

DEGREES TO

ANCE

EXPERIMENTAL

HOUSE 5 : EXPERIMENTAL

10 DEGREES TO SUNDANCE

> STILETTO NYC

SEE ALSO:
> MTV VIDEO MUSIC AWARDS : BEST NEW ARTIST CATEGORY 212

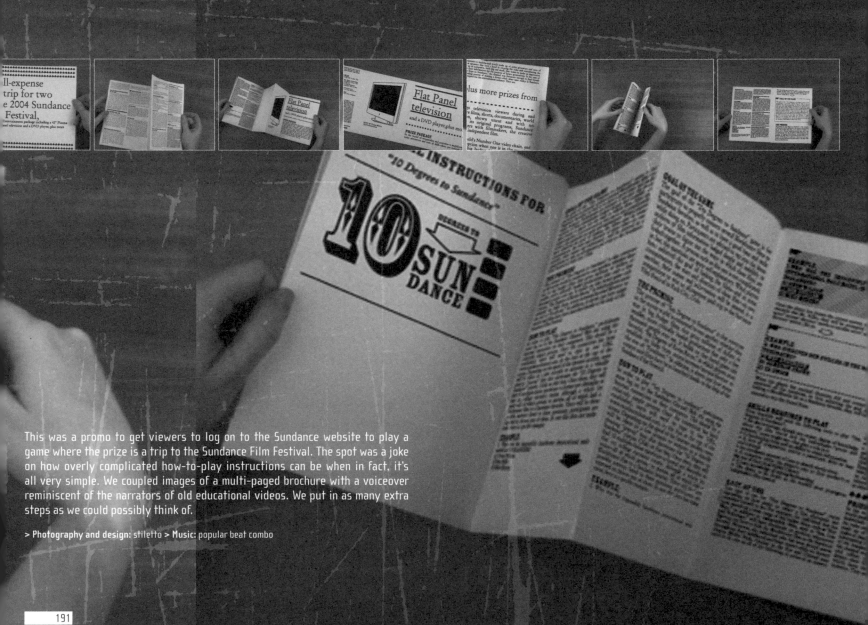

This was a promo to get viewers to log on to the Sundance website to play a game where the prize is a trip to the Sundance Film Festival. The spot was a joke on how overly complicated how-to-play instructions can be when in fact, it's all very simple. We coupled images of a multi-paged brochure with a voiceover reminiscent of the narrators of old educational videos. We put in as many extra steps as we could possibly think of.

> **Photography and design:** stiletto > **Music:** popular beat combo

> STILETTO NYC

Stiletto nyc is the graphic design studio of Julie Hirschfeld and Stefanie Barth. In 2000, they compiled and edited *Pause: 59 Minutes Of Motion Graphics*, a book chronicling the history of the medium and showcasing some of the field's best work, published by Calman & King, London. The success of the book cemented the partnership and established a consolidated studio in New York. The two work on projects spanning motion graphics, live action and print design. They have worked with such clients as MTV, Nike, German music television channel VIVA Plus, USA Networks, RCA Records, HBO, architect Andrea Tognon, Sundance Channel, Area and *Res* magazines. Stiletto has been featured in *The Face*, *Wallpaper**, *i-D*. magazine's "40 Under 30" issue and in Restart: New Systems in Graphic Design, published by Universe. They have won two Art Directors' Club awards for their motion graphics for MTV. A survey of their projects, both in motion and in print, is part of the book *Fresh Dialogue*, featuring experimental design studios and published by Princeton Architectural Press in association with the American Institute of Graphic Arts.

IdN: Do you think MTV can be considered as short film?

SNYC: We try to approach all of our jobs as short films at some level. This is what keeps our work interesting for us.

IdN: The style of the *10 Degrees To Sundance* is really unique. What made you choose this method of filming?

SNYC: The task was originally really literal: to promote a game online where you can win tickets to the festival. The game was actually online, but we were inspired by old board-game-style rule sheets that tend to be overly complicated. We chose to film the piece in stop motion, which added to the overall quirkiness of the approach.

IdN: Is there special meaning behind the title?

SNYC: That was actually the title the Sundance Channel gave us.

IdN: Describe your favourite movie-viewing venue.

SNYC: The Sunshine Theater in the Lower East Side.

IdN: What is your favourite movie?

SNYC: For right now (for Stefanie) it's *Hero* or *Star Wars* (the original).

IdN: How would you define the differences between film and movies?

SNYC: I never knew people differentiated.

IdN: Where would you most like to see your work screened?

SNYC: In an exhibition, possibly, or in a store projection. Basically, anywhere where you have a nice space and a great wall to project the work onto.

IdN: How do you feel about the increasing popularity of short film as a genre?

SNYC: I think it's great if companies start to commission more and more short films. That allows us all to work on these interesting projects.

IdN: If you could use a specific item to represent the categories drama, fantasy, sci-fi, experimental and documentary, what would you choose?

SNYC: Fantasy and experimental sound interesting as categories. We like to work with the idea of dreamscapes, and surreal scenarios. That leaves a lot of freedom for the mind to go ahead and experiment.

HOUSE 5 : EXPERIMENTAL
BQSEA

> TRONIC STUDIO

SEE ALSO:
> REGRET 216

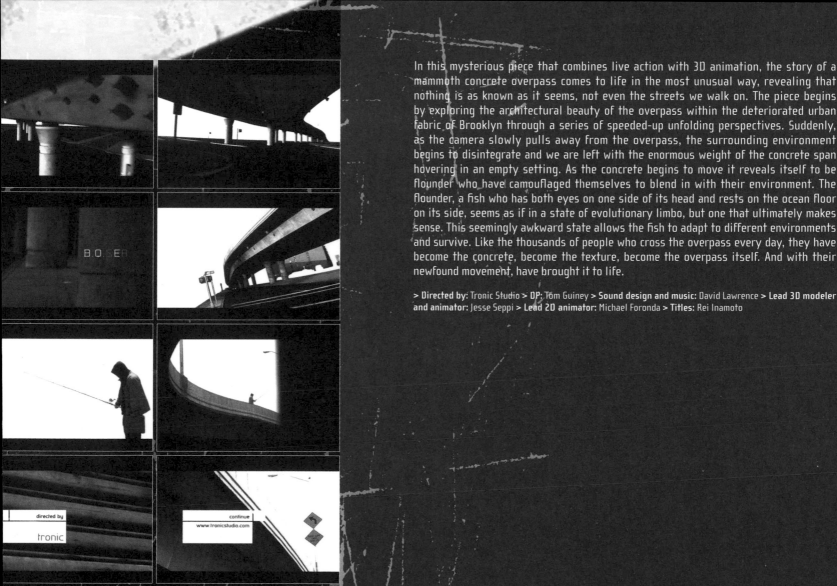

In this mysterious piece that combines live action with 3D animation, the story of a mammoth concrete overpass comes to life in the most unusual way, revealing that nothing is as known as it seems, not even the streets we walk on. The piece begins by exploring the architectural beauty of the overpass within the deteriorated urban fabric of Brooklyn through a series of speeded-up unfolding perspectives. Suddenly, as the camera slowly pulls away from the overpass, the surrounding environment begins to disintegrate and we are left with the enormous weight of the concrete span hovering in an empty setting. As the concrete begins to move it reveals itself to be flounder who have camouflaged themselves to blend in with their environment. The flounder, a fish who has both eyes on one side of its head and rests on the ocean floor on its side, seems as if in a state of evolutionary limbo, but one that ultimately makes sense. This seemingly awkward state allows the fish to adapt to different environments and survive. Like the thousands of people who cross the overpass every day, they have become the concrete, become the texture, become the overpass itself. And with their newfound movement, have brought it to life.

> **Directed by:** Tronic Studio > **DP:** Tom Guiney > **Sound design and music:** David Lawrence > **Lead 3D modeler and animator:** Jesse Seppi > **Lead 2D animator:** Michael Foronda > **Titles:** Rei Inamoto

> TRONIC STUDIO

Tronic Studio is a New York City directing, design and animation studio founded in the Spring of 2001 by Columbia Architecture graduates Jesse Seppi and Vivian Rosenthal. Their work moves between broadcast, film and installation design. They've delivered unique digital visions for both RES and Creative Review, directed and animated spots for Nike, Fuse, MTV, the Fine Living Network and NEC, conceived and executed projects for Diesel, GE and Wired (in store) and Nike (online) and, in general, have worked to eliminate lines delineating one form of creative media output from another.

www.tronicstudio.com

IdN: How did you become involved in Nike's "Art Of Speed" project?

TS: Tronic has been working with Nike for over two years creating 3D models of their products, including sneakers, watches and MP3 players. "The Art of Speed" was a natural extension of the work we had been doing with Nike. It was an opportunity to create a short CG film that explored the physical and psychological effects of speed on the body.

IdN: Describe your favourite movie-viewing venue.

TS: On my couch in my house.

IdN: What is your favourite movie?

TS: There are a many, but some of the favourites are *Fight Club, Rivers And Tides, Vanilla Sky, Ghost In The Shell* ...

IdN: How would you define the differences between film and movie?

TS: The word movie connotes that which is about entertainment. Film refers more to experimentation.

IdN: Where would you most like to see your work screened?

TS: So far, the most exciting screening of Tronic's work has been at ResFest; it is terrific to see the work on that large a scale, with a big audience.

IdN: The popularity of short film is growing, with an increasing number of festivals and competitions hosting the genre. How do you feel about this and what can be done to increase the exposure even further?

TS: It's good that there's more competition. It means that the level of sophistication and quality should increase, which raises the bar for the directors and animators, which we see as a positive thing. A very effective way to increase short-film exposure is to continue to have brands sponsor the creation of short films.

IdN: If you could use specific items to represent the categories drama, fantasy, sci-fi, experimental and documentary, what would you choose?

TS: Drama – people; fantasy – abstract landscapes; sci-fi – cyborgs; experimental – architecture; documentary – cameras. Those are just the first words that come to mind when I think of those categories. To me, they have become synonymous with each other.

There are two sides to every story, two points of view. *Dual/Duel* pushes the boundaries of what is reality and what is fiction by blurring the thin line that separates them. The film is viewed from an "observers" perspective and features multiple endings should the main character have decided differently while escaping an unseen foe. What is her fate, what is her destiny?

> **Directed by:** Rob Chiu > **Photography and Edited by:** Rob Chiu > **Motion Graphics by:** The Ronin
> **Starring:** Rachel Reid > **Music by:** Diagram of Suburban Chaos

HOUSE 5 : EXPERIMENTAL
DUAL/DUEL

> THE RONIN

DUAL MK III
AUTHENTICATE
ORIGINATION

ility phase 01

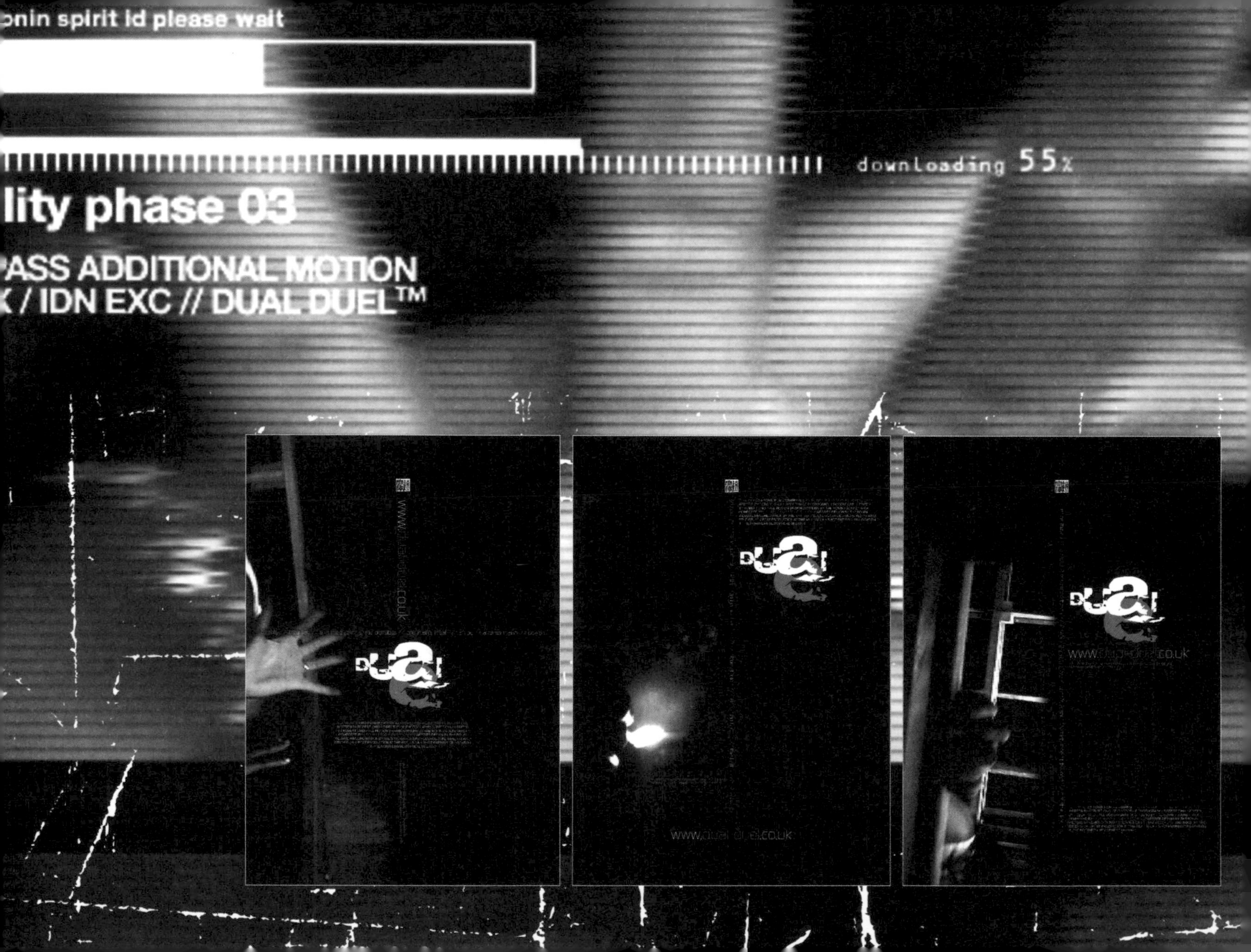

onin spirit id please wait
downloading 55%
lity phase 03
ASS ADDITIONAL MOTION
/ IDN EXC // DUAL DUEL™
www.dualduel.co.uk
www.dualduel.co.uk
www.dualduel.co.uk

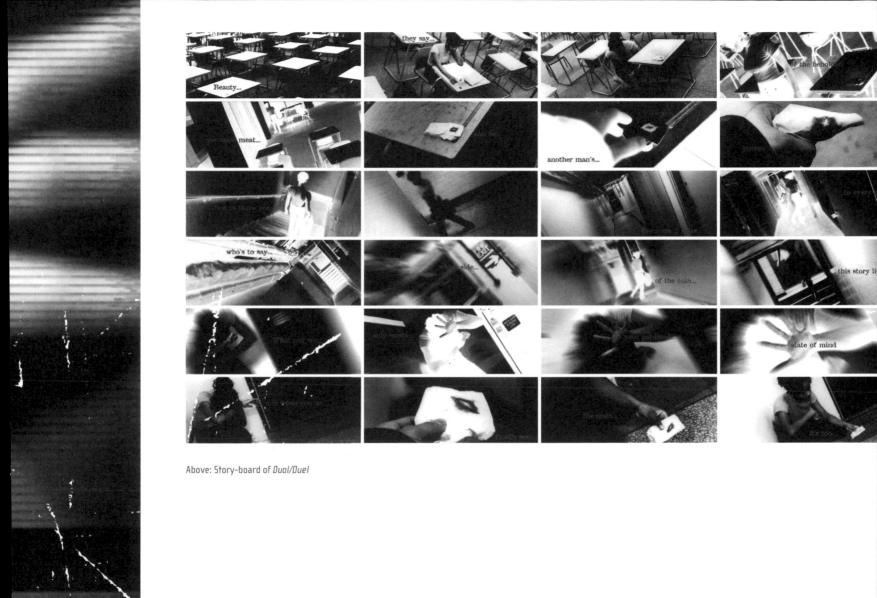

Above: Story-board of *Dual/Duel*

> THE RONIN

Rob Chiu set up The Ronin as a motion graphics studio in 2000. After being awarded by Output 03 for his short personal film – *Journey* he quickly built up an impressive body of work. Three of Robs films have been archived by the British Film Institute and he has also presented work at the ICA, BD4D, Digital Arts World and Media Elements. His short animation for Channel 4 UK – *Dimensions* (part of the Animated Minds series), has won two awards and has also been played at a number of high profile film festivals including ResFest and Edinburgh. Robs work was a part of the first international graphic design exhibition by Computer Love in Brussels in 2003 and has appeared in publications such as *Grafik, Computer Arts, Digit* and *Hype* Magazine.

IdN: What triggers you having such a great passion toward short filmmaking?

RC: When I hear certain types of music I see images. I would say that my passion comes from a piece of music that leads to all sorts of emotions and imagery trying to escape my head... I feel like I have a lot of sadness and joy to share which is usually initially stirred up by a piece of music which will lead to me forming an idea or a treatment...

IdN: The style and story behind the Dual/Duel is really unique, why you chose this filming method/way of story telling?

RC: I think my style/method is born out of having no prior experience, no formal training in motion of film and also out of a lack of tools such as 35mm film, actors etc... As all my work so far has been on DV and edited on a desktop computer the style has evolved as a result of trying to make the best film possible with the tools given. If I was to shoot on 35mm with camera cranes etc and have access to actors and scripts and edit on an Avid or something then I think that maybe my style would have been totally different. My style evolves from piece to piece. Each film is a learning process which I take to the next film and so on... My style is in progress.

The story for *Dual/Duel* came from a project I did at college for which I formed a load of storyboards etc using photography and typography. It was entitled Consuming Passions so I devised a story consisting of a person who is consumed with passion for someone or something. I wanted to show how people view situations differently. The text reflected this along with the narrative of the photographs. A few years later when I decided to take the project into film I thought it would be good to give the piece multiple endings to show how things could have been. This in addition to the original concept of seeing things from different perspectives kind of all meshed together really well and actually gave the film its name *Dual*. This then led to me thinking of the title *Dual/Duel* because of the perspective you can take that the girl is being pursued!

IdN: Describe your most favourite movie-viewing place.

RC: Would have to be the cinema. I love the excitement of going to see a brand new film but I also love DVD for the quality and extras!

IdN: What is your favourite movie?

RC: Of all time? That's a really hard question... Can I choose more than 1? Ok... In no particular order... My all time favourites would have to be... *ET* (Steven Spielberg 1982), *Star Wars – A New Hope* (George Lucas 1977)... and *The Thin Red Line* (Terrence Malik 1998), for the sheer beauty and power of it...

IdN: How would you define the differences between film and movie?

RC: A film is forever... A movie is for Christmas.

IdN: How and where would be your favourite place for your works' screening?

RC: I like to see my films in a cinema transferred to 35mm... This has happened three times so far and always excites me just before I go to see it... Its good to sit in an audience where no one knows who you are and that you made the piece! Its good to hear what people say!

IdN: The popularity of short film is getting higher and higher, more and more competition of short film is being host. As a creator of short film, how you feel about that?

RC: I think it is good... It keeps you as a film maker on your toes... I am always looking for new ways of approaching something so that it can be different to whatever else is going on out there! If there was no competition it is easy to get complacent and not push boundaries. Its a good time for film makers now with all the technology so cheap compared to ten years ago! I think this will bring about a lot of crap films but will also launch some undiscovered gems. I believe the next Spielberg or Scorsese will come from the humble beginnings of digital film making. The bedroom film maker as I call it... Just like the musicians of today started with a Casio and a sampler in the back bedroom!

IdN: From your point of view what would be the most effective and useful way allow more and more short film exposure?

RC: When I was young.. Back in the seventies, there used to be short films playing before full length features at the cinemas. I think that the cinemas and multiplexes need to bring this format back to encourage the upcoming directors to be the next generation of film makers! Travelling Film Festivals such as ResFest are also really great and get your work shown in countries you wouldn't normally have thought possible! But the ultimate in maximum exposure has got to be via the internet! You just cant beat it!! The cheaper digital storage and bandwidth becomes the more high quality movies will appear online!

IdN: If you could use a specific item to represent following categories, drama, fantasy, sci-fi, experimental and documentary. What would be your choice and why?

RC: Hmmmm.... Drama – *24* Season 1 DVD Box Set – Doesn't get much better than this! Fantasy – Secret of Mana SNES cart – The ultimate in Fantasy story telling! Sci-Fi - Boba Fett Action Figure – Represents everything cool about Sci-Fi! Experimental – An iPod – for a massive catalog of music to help inspire a new way of story telling. Documentary – 3CCD DV Camera – For the sheer immediacy of it.

FASTER WAY TO START THE DAY

> HONEST

SEE ALSO :
> I'M FALLING FOREVER   086

For Nike's "You're Faster Than You Think" campaign, they asked seven directors to create a two- to four-minute film that both touches on the themes of the campaign as well as expands it into areas that people might be surprised by. We created a film, *Best Way To Start The Day*, that follows four characters as they wake up and get ready to go out in the morning. Unbeknownst to them, they are racing against each other to see who gets out the door first.

> **Directd by:** HONEST > **Written by:** HONEST > **Cast:** Paul Raff – Unemployed Guy / Gary Welz – Professor / Nicole Tozzi – Entrepreneur / Alex Valente – Lawyer / Ron Morelli – Unemployed Guy's Friend > **Produced by:** Sabrina Tubio-Cid > **Edited by:** HONEST > **Original Music by:** Jose Ayala > **Sound Design by:** David Reid and ... > **Crew:** Director of Photography – Scott Beardslee / Assistant Director – Sabrina Tubio-Cid / Gaffer – Ivan Grboric / Key Grip – Jake Sofer / Best Boy Grip – Aida Artieda / Swing – Matt Cross / 1st AC – Jen Scarlotta / Sound Recordists – John Issac, Jack Hutson / Production Designer – Tora Peterson / Art Director – Shahar Yannay / Production Assistant – Ron Morelli / Production Assistant – Tom Carley / Production Assistant – Johnathan Swafford > **Casting by:** Doreen Frumkin > **Production Management:** HONEST > **Graphics by:** HONEST > **Camera Packages:** Charlie Beyer > **Special thanks:** Chiara Alberetti, Annie Campbell, Antoinnette Advento, Gregory Murnion, Gisellah Harvey, Kitty, Rory Rubin, Greg Brunkalla, and Sean Dougherty

HOUSE 5 : EXPERIMENTAL
FUTURE "CUT COPY"

> SOFT CITIZEN

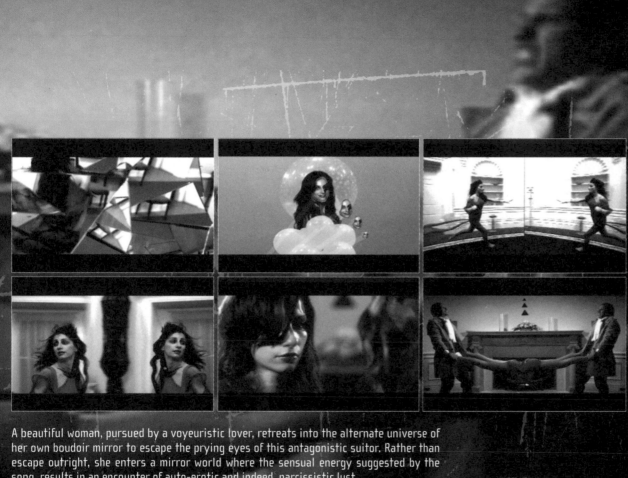

A beautiful woman, pursued by a voyeuristic lover, retreats into the alternate universe of her own boudoir mirror to escape the prying eyes of this antagonistic suitor. Rather than escape outright, she enters a mirror world where the sensual energy suggested by the song, results in an encounter of auto-erotic and indeed, narcissistic lust.

> Canada | 2004 | 3:33 > **Production company:** Soft Citizen > **Director:** Jaron Albertin > **Executive producers:** Sandy Hunter and Jamie Watson > **Record co:** Modular People

> SOFT CITIZEN

The newest company nestled beneath the Radke Films umbrella is Soft Citizen, a dedicated music-video production company. Run by Sandy Hunter (also *Res* magazine's and ResFest's Canadian operative) and producer Jamie Watson, Soft Citizen was launched in the autumn of 2003 with the intention of producing both Canadian and international videos for music talents from both the realms of the underground and more mainstream fare.

Soft Citizen's recent work includes director Jason MacFarlane's *Catch A Moment In Time* for Canadian pop artist Mocky, and Jaron Albertin's *7 Minutes* for the progressively electronic artist Circlesquare. The cadre of directors working through Soft Citizen have already produced music videos for Kid Koala, Badly Drawn Boy, Grandaddy, Solvent, Ascii Disko, Zero 7 and Hayden. Styles range from comedic live action, innovative performances, cutting-edge digital techniques and classic animation.

IdN: What triggered your passion for short-film-making?

JA: Since I was little I've been into film-making. It's not so much about definitive narrative structure for me, but this experimental part of film that I don't think has been tapped into entirely. In the world at the moment, it's such a powerful medium it's scary. It's shaping society – look at the United States.

IdN: How did you develop your style?

JA: I try to reflect exactly what comes into my mind. Sometimes I think, "Well, okay, F**k, I can't roll with that", but then I try not to worry about it. Sometimes my own work makes me cringe. It's at this point that I take it a step further. Then I get my kicks out of it.

IdN: Describe your favourite movie-viewing venue.

JA: Well, I always enjoy going to the theatres.

IdN: What is your favourite movie?

JA: I don't have one favourite, but it would be beautiful to say I loved one so much. Right now, *Songs From The Second Floor* is my favourite. I love the colour palette and the fact that he sticks to his basis.

IdN: How would you define the differences between film and movies?

JA: Well, film for me is experimental. With movies, I feel you are limited by structure. Movies are meant for entertainment, but film is an open palette.

IdN: Where would you most like to see your work screened?

JA: It wouldn't be about my work specifically, but I see a small rooftop festival being nice: a community of creative people all drinking and sleeping with each other.

IdN: How do you feel about the growing popularity of short film as a genre?

JA: Well, I think the access given to creative projects from the mainstream is getting less and less. People are looking more and more for less commercial projects. Short films at the moment are a great outlet for free creative reign, and at the same time it doesn't take a lot of resources to make them manageable. I see these festivals popping up all over. I don't think television is the answer for short films. It's all about the event and a community of the people getting together.

HOUSE 5 : EXPERIMENTAL
MSN

> HISAKO HIRAI / FABRICA

SEE ALSO:
> FREE TIBET 130

This movie was made for MSN competition.

> Illustration and Motion Graphic Design by: Hisako Hirai
> Music by: Andres Reymondes Mutti

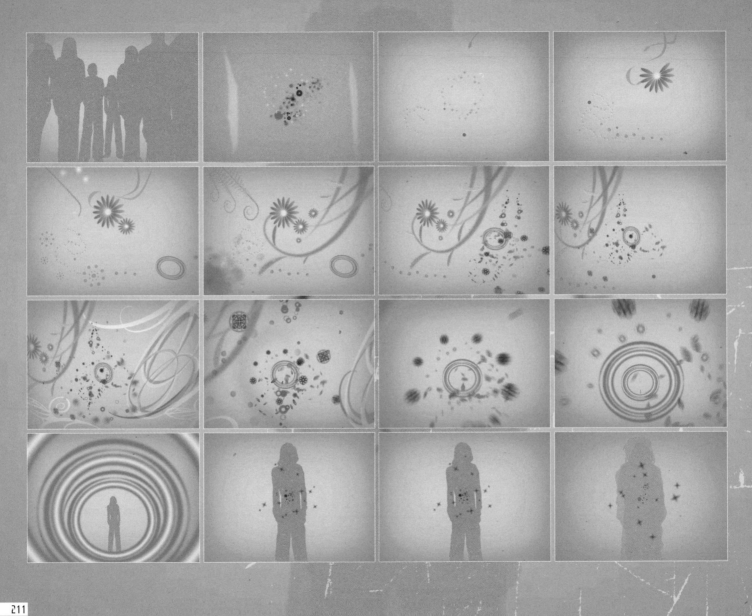

MTV VIDEO MUSIC AWARDS : BEST NEW ARTIST CATEGORY

> STILETTO NYC

SEE ALSO:
> 10 DEGREES TO SUNDANCE 190

MTV commissioned different studios to do parts of the VMA identity, recalling the station's more experimental early days. We were assigned a 15-second title sequence for best new artist in a music video. In response, we wanted to do something simple and appropriate to youth culture. Since the video music awards reflect on the achievements of the previous year, we filmed a simple sequence and played it backwards, i.e. looking back on something that was once fresh and new, but has since left its mark.

> **MTV video music awards:** Best new artist category design/Creative Direction / Director: stiletto
> **Director of photography:** Matthew Beals > **Animation / edit:** Ultrabland > **Music:** Trevor Sias

Full spread: *MTV Video Music Awards : Best New Artist Category*'s behind the scene

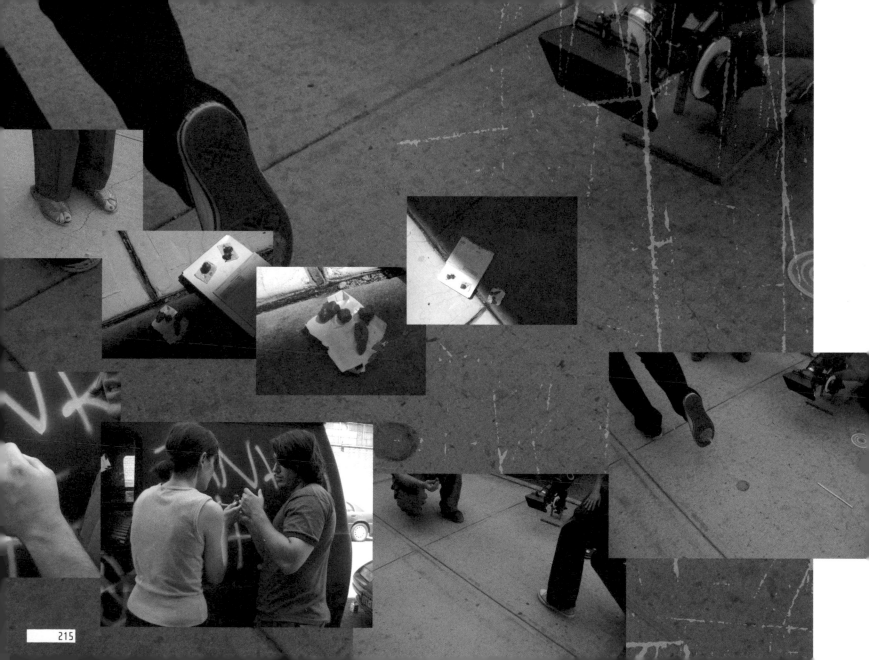

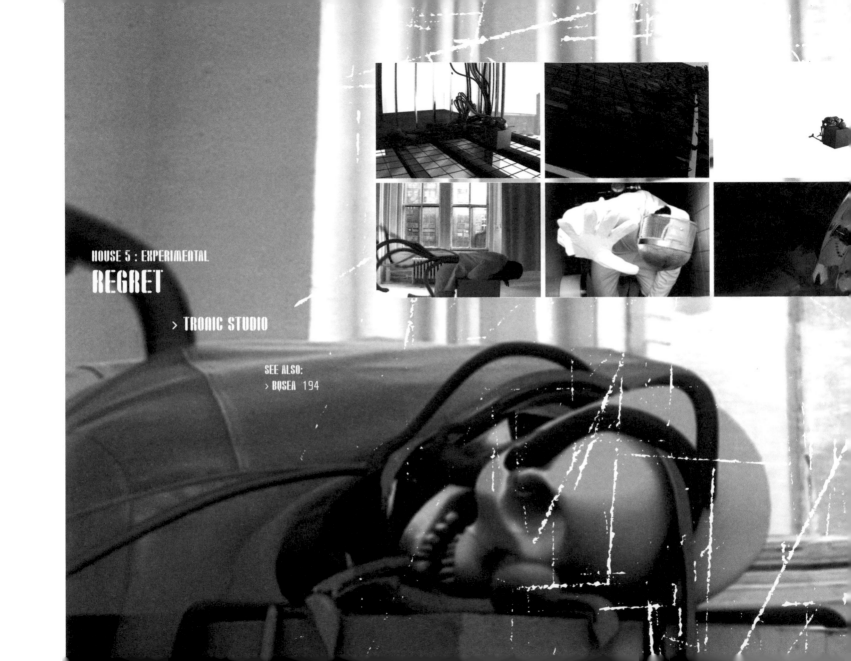

HOUSE 5 : EXPERIMENTAL
REGRET

> TRONIC STUDIO

SEE ALSO:
> BQSEA 194

Tronic was commissioned by Tekko to create a short film. The result was a hybrid live-action and CG short that examines one man's relation of regret through the eyes of a fencer. His anatomy and the architecture begin to fuse into one, as he is forced to confront flying tiles and animated vascular systems.

> **Directed by:** Tronic Studio > **DP:** Rod Lamborn > **Sound design and music:** Q Department > **Lead 3D modeler and animator:** Jesse Seppi > **Second 3D modeler and animator:** Gaspard Giroud

HOUSE 5 : EXPERIMENTAL

RESFEST 2004 OPENING FILM

> MOTION THEORY

SEE ALSO :
> GETTING AWAY WITH MURDER 016

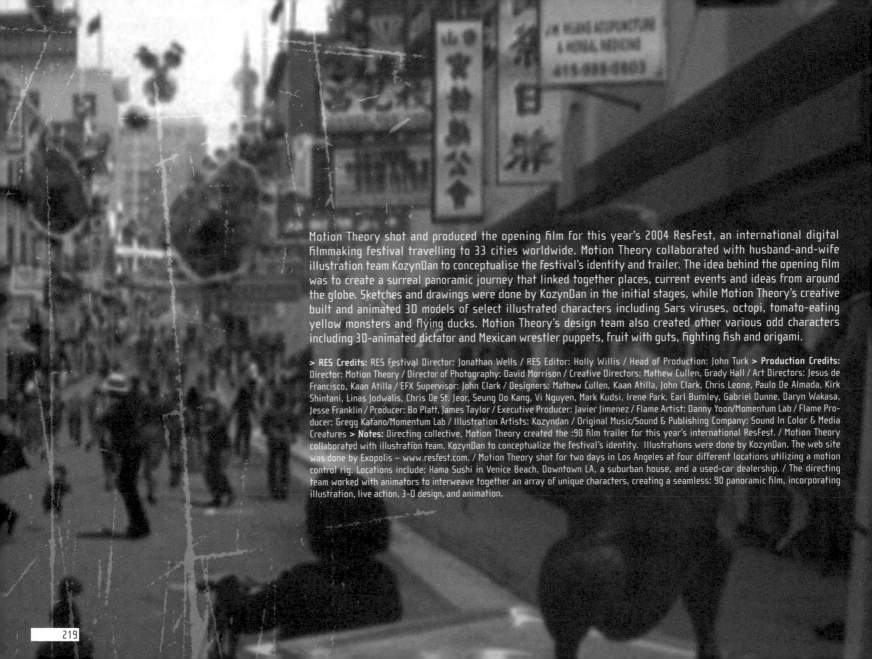

Motion Theory shot and produced the opening film for this year's 2004 ResFest, an international digital filmmaking festival travelling to 33 cities worldwide. Motion Theory collaborated with husband-and-wife illustration team KozynDan to conceptualise the festival's identity and trailer. The idea behind the opening film was to create a surreal panoramic journey that linked together places, current events and ideas from around the globe. Sketches and drawings were done by KozynDan in the initial stages, while Motion Theory's creative built and animated 3D models of select illustrated characters including Sars viruses, octopi, tomato-eating yellow monsters and flying ducks. Motion Theory's design team also created other various odd characters including 3D-animated dictator and Mexican wrestler puppets, fruit with guts, fighting fish and origami.

> RES Credits: RES Festival Director: Jonathan Wells / RES Editor: Holly Willis / Head of Production: John Turk **> Production Credits:** Director: Motion Theory / Director of Photography: David Morrison / Creative Directors: Mathew Cullen, Grady Hall / Art Directors: Jesus de Francisco, Kaan Atilla / EFX Supervisor: John Clark / Designers: Mathew Cullen, Kaan Atilla, John Clark, Chris Leone, Paulo De Almada, Kirk Shintani, Linas Jodwalis, Chris De St. Jeor, Seung Do Kang, Vi Nguyen, Mark Kudsi, Irene Park, Earl Burnley, Gabriel Dunne, Daryn Wakasa, Jesse Franklin / Producer: Bo Platt, James Taylor / Executive Producer: Javier Jimenez / Flame Artist: Danny Yoon/Momentum Lab / Flame Producer: Gregg Katano/Momentum Lab / Illustration Artists: Kozyndan / Original Music/Sound & Publishing Company: Sound In Color & Media Creatures **> Notes:** Directing collective, Motion Theory created the :90 film trailer for this year's international ResFest. / Motion Theory collaborated with illustration team, KozynDan to conceptualize the festival's identity. Illustrations were done by KozynDan. The web site was done by Exopolis – www.resfest.com. / Motion Theory shot for two days in Los Angeles at four different locations utilizing a motion control rig. Locations include: Hama Sushi in Venice Beach, Downtown LA, a suburban house, and a used-car dealership. / The directing team worked with animators to interweave together an array of unique characters, creating a seamless :90 panoramic film, incorporating illustration, live action, 3-D design, and animation.

Full spread: *ResFest 2004*
Opening Film's behind scene.

HOUSE 5 : EXPERIMENTAL
STROKES

> XAVIER COOK

The story of an 80-year-old fluffer and his 50 years as an integral part of the adult-entertainment industry.

> **Written and Directed by:** Xavier Cook > **Produced by:** Julien Cook > **Cameraman:** Yong Hong Zhong > **Actors Credits:** Strokes: Xavier Cook / Director: Johnny Winningham / Male Porn Actor: Drew Marks / Female Porn Actress: Michelle McKay / Background players: Micheal Anthony Snowden, Julien Cook, Kari Bavasso, Marissa Totaro > **Original Music:** "When you can't get it up" / Written and produced by: Patrick Griffin and Julien Cook / Performed by: Iliana Griffin

Xavier Cook, 32, has been a professional comedy writer for the past 10 years. He has contributed material for the Wayans Bros. show and Mad TV for several seasons. Most recently, he co-wrote the movie *White Chicks*.

IdN: What triggered your passion for short-film-making?

XC: Ever since I was a kid I have loved shorts and sketch comedy. I also have a short attention span. So, shorts are a great way for me to explore a funny concept and then get out of it before I get bored with it.

IdN: Do you think that a site like ifilm is useful? How does it help your career development?

XC: ifilm and sites like it are a short-film-maker's dream. They give you the potential to reach people all around the world. They also allow you to get feedback, even though it's not always good.

IdN: The style and story behind *Strokes* is very original. Why did you choose this method of telling the story?

XC: I wanted the character *Strokes* to be an old, hard-working black man, who just happens to be a fluffer. He could be fluffing or fixing cars. All that matters to him is doing good and having pride in his work. I thought it was funny because he looks like the last person in the world who would have a job in the porn business. When I shot it, I wanted as little camera movement as possible so that the viewer would be like a fly on the wall

IdN: What is your favourite movie?

XC: *Welcome To The Dollhouse.*

IdN: Where would you most like to see your work screened?

XC: My favourite places are sites such as ifilm or short-film festivals. Your films are viewed by people who are looking for something different and they might appreciate some of the chances the filmmakers are taking more than the average person.

IdN: How do you feel about the increased popularity of short film?

XC: I think the more competition the better. It pushes you to be more creative and makes you better at your craft. As for more exposure, I think it will come the more people realise the short-film-makers of today are the big-film-makers of tomorrow.

HOUSE 5 : EXPERIMENTAL

TEO 12

> REI INAMARO

SEE ALSO:
> AICP 2001 164   > AICP 2002 166

TED – a famed Technology, Entertainment, Design conference conceived by information-design guru Richard Saul Wurman – celebrated its 12th event in 2002. To serve the opening of the event as well as individual sessions, the opening title was created in order to visually introduce the event. Using filmstrips as a visual device to present 12 distinct themes, the opening title sequence creates a flipbook-like effect for the audience on screen. Individual vignettes then introduce each session – themed "The Design Of Animals", "The Design Of The Car", "The Design Of Sensuality", etc.

> **Director:** Rei Inamoto > **Designers:** Jerome Austria, David Morrow, Garry Waller > **Special Effects Artist:** Danny Gonzalez > **Editor:** Brandon Werner > **Agency:** R/GA

THE CUBE

> BEN TSENG / FABRICA

SEE ALSO:
> THIS IS THE CREATURE INSIDE 156

A trailer for the animation *The Cube*

> **Director:** Ben Tseng Ho Fung
> **Music by:** Andres Reymondes Mutti

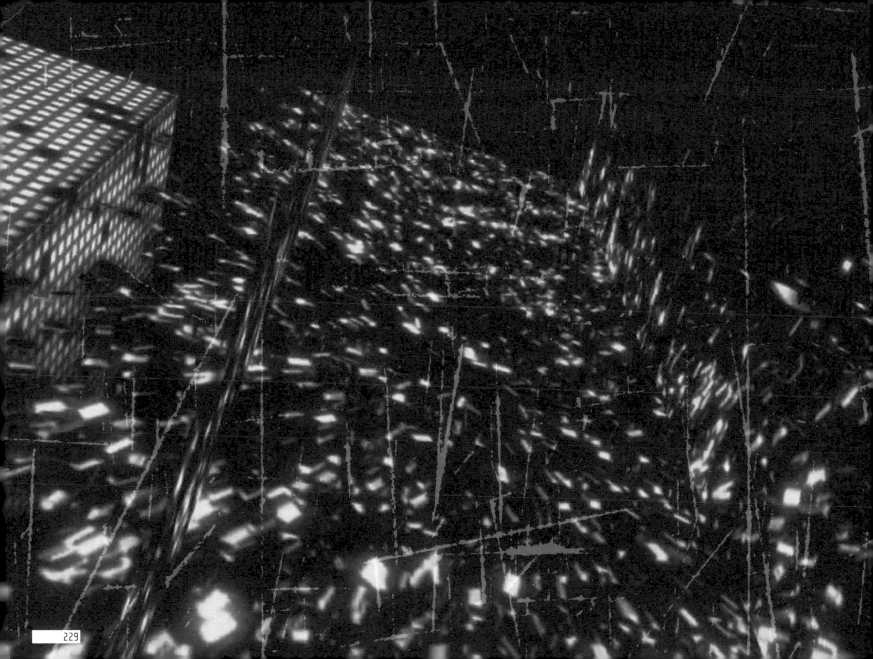

INDEX

THE PUBLISHER OF IdN MAGAZINE PRESENTS
A SYSTEMS DESIGN LIMITED PRODUCTION SHOP C 5-9 GRESSON STREET WANCHAI HONG KONG
TEL 852 2528 5744 FAX 852 2529 1296 EMAIL INFO@IDNWORLD.COM URL WWW.IDNWORLD.COM

"FLIPS 8 : MOVIEW" ISBN 988-98097-3-7 2004 FIRST EDITION

PUBLISHER LAURENCE NG DIRECTOR CHRIS NG EDITOR BILL CRANFIELD ASSISTANT EDITOR CHLOÉ TANG
EDITORIAL ASSISTANT ALVA WONG SENIOR DESIGNER BRYAN LEUNG PR EXECUTIVE KAMAN WONG
CIRCULATION MANAGER FLORA KWOK PRODUCTION MANAGER NGAN KWOK MAN

DVD-ROM specifications >>>

| DVD VIDEO | ALL | MPEG-2 | NTSC | COLOUR STEREO |